Bounce-back Ability

Developing Resilience on the Rollercoaster of Life

Helen Turier

www.90daybooks.com

First published in Great Britain in 2012 by 90-Day Books, a trading name of Meaningful Goals Ltd., Sussex, England. www.90daybooks.com

Copyright © 2012 by Helen Turier, all rights reserved.

Helen Turier has asserted her right under the Copyright, Designs and Patents Act 1988 to be identified as the author of this work.

No part of this book may be used or reproduced, stored in a retrieval system, or transmitted in any form or any means, electronic, mechanical, photocopying, recording, scanning, or otherwise, except as permitted by the Copyright, Designs and Patents Act 1988, without either the prior written permission of the publisher or the author.

This book is sold subject to the condition that it shall not, by way of trade or otherwise, be lent, resold, hired out, or otherwise circulated without the publisher's prior consent in any form of binding or cover other than that in which it is published and without a similar condition, including this condition, being imposed on the subsequent purchaser.

Limit of Liability/Disclaimer of Warranty: While the publisher and author have used their best efforts in preparing this book, they make no representations or warranties with respect to the accuracy or completeness of the contents of this book and specifically disclaim any implied warranties of merchantability or fitness for a particular purpose. The advice and strategies contained herein may not be suitable for your situation. Neither the publisher nor author shall be liable for any loss of profit or any other commercial damages, including but not limited to special, incidental, consequential, or other damages.

Author's photograph by Kim Rix, Wedding & Portrait Photographer
www.kimrixphotography.co.uk

Front cover layout and design by Russell Knight Design
www.russellknight.co.uk

Book interior design and layout by Kevin Bermingham, 90-Day Books.

Diagrams by Helen Turier.

British Library Cataloguing in Publication Data.
A catalogue record for this book is available from the British Library.

V2-Paperback edition

ISBN 978-1-908101-08-2

1. Self-Improvement

Acknowledgements

This book would still be in the planning stages if Kevin Bermingham, the *"90-Day Guy"*, hadn't invited me onto his 90-Day Books Programme. Writing this book has been an amazing experience. Not least, because I was a member of his 90-Day Books Group. Full of brilliant people; each of whom succeeded in writing their own book within the same ninety days. Thank goodness for our Facebook group, those encouraging posts really kept me on track when I needed it most. The mutual support and encouragement provided by Kevin and the group really helped me to succeed.

Ever since I first told them that I was writing a book, my kids Joshua, Victoria and Georgina, have been wonderfully supportive and encouraging. Thank you for pulling together and helping out, so I could get my writing done. You are amazing and I am very proud of you.

Finally, thank you to my team of manuscript reviewers, who freely donated their time and worked hard to get their comments on the drafts back to me so promptly – you know who you are! You are all stars.

Some Kind Words

"After eighteen months dealing with a marriage split, I was delighted to read Helen Turier's book and discover that emotional resilience really is the key to true personal happiness. For others in the same position as me, "Bounce-back Ability: Developing Resilience on the Rollercoaster of Life", provides an excellent grounding and springboard for further "directed" self-development. I have come such a long way and have now developed my own emotional resilience. I will definitely keep this book close at hand for those inevitable low days when I just need that extra bit of motivation."

Hazel Biggs

"I really enjoyed Helen's workshop, it gave me lots of ideas to take back to work and also to use in my life in general."

Nicola Hughes

"I've been on one of Helen's workshops. She's really inspiring - you'll have fun, think hard, and come out with some great ideas and plans tailored just for you!"

Julie Joyce

Contents

Introduction	9
Change is a fact of life	19
Are you a victim, or survivor?	33
The future is bright, the future is yours!	55
Take one step at a time towards your goals	73
Celebrate your successes and nurture an attitude of gratitude	97
Be connected and supported	109
Nurture your mind, body and spirit	125
And finally…	159
Personal Bounce-back Ability Plan	163
B.O.U.N.C.E. The Bounce-back Ability Tool Kit	167
Important Notice	171
Bibliography	175
Useful Websites	179
About The Author	183
Cultive8	189

Introduction

Do you sometimes feel like your life is a rollercoaster? Has your life been feeling like its one saga or drama after another? Has this turbulent ride through life left you feeling frazzled and worn out? Do you wish for a smoother calmer ride on life's rollercoaster?

That is exactly how I felt after a number of emotionally turbulent years. The best way that I can find to describe how I felt, is that it was as if I had lost my 'bounce' and wasn't sure how to go about getting it back again.

The aim of this book is to share with you how I rediscovered my bounce back, what I have learnt about resilience, and my tips for handling life's ups and downs. I hope the book can help you too, if you are experiencing similar feelings and that it will give you tips, inspiration and guidance on "Bounce-back Ability: Developing resilience on the rollercoaster of life".

My recent "*Annus Horribilis*" came 5 years ago. In the space of a year, two loved ones lost their battles with cancer, I moved house, my relationship broke down, and I changed career. It seemed to me, during that year to eighteen-month period, that each time I started to recover; life dealt yet another blow. This emotional rollercoaster left me feeling unsure of my own abilities; my self-belief and my confidence were drained.

I was also unsure of my direction or my goals. I wasn't depressed, but I also wasn't myself. I literally felt that life had knocked the bounce out of me.

I have always considered myself very capable of coping with life's ups and downs. After all, I have been juggling work and being a lone parent to twin girls and their older brother for 15 years. I have struggled with living on social welfare/benefits when my children were tiny, and then worked hard to get back into full-time employment. I had been promoted rapidly at work, and even held director positions on the boards of two companies within 5 years of returning to work. I'd also successfully got myself out of rented accommodation and onto the property ladder. All the time, handling all the usual ups and downs of modern life such as family issues, school changes, kids growing up, friends and family members going through divorce etc.

So as far as I was concerned, I had lots of evidence to support my personal theory that, because I had coped before, I should be coping now. Clearly though, I was not doing as well as I would have liked.

The questions I asked myself at this point were; "What was different this time?" And, "How had I coped before and how could I cope better this time?" Then, the really important one, "How was I going to get my bounce back?"

Back in 2008, I was running a busy reflexology practice, and noted that a significant number of clients had come to reflexology as a way to cope more effectively with stress, as stress was affecting their wellbeing and health.

This stimulated my interest in stress and, in particular, why people cope well with stress and why others find stress more debilitating.

My previous career as a nurse, years earlier, had given me a wealth of knowledge on stress and its effects on mind and body. During that time, I had seen many real life examples of people who had struggled against adversity and survived. I knew that these people were resilient and what I wanted to understand was what made some people more resilient than others? And, could resilience be developed in order to protect us from the stresses and strains of modern life?

Resilience, to put it simply, is the ability to bounce back in the face of adversity. At www.dictionary.com, resilience is defined as:

> *'The power or ability to return to the original form after being bent, compressed or stretched, the ability to recover readily from adversity.'*

Resilience is not a personality trait that some people have and others do not have. It is a combination of behaviours, thoughts, and actions that can be learned and developed by all of us. By becoming more resilient, we learn to adapt well with the twists and turns of the rollercoaster of life.

Resilience has become the focus of many psychological studies. Most prominently was research by Werner & Smith in 1955, which centred on children, born in that year and who were followed until their 40th birthdays. The lives of these children saw them struggling with poverty, parental difficulties, illness and other issues. Many of these children went on to do well in spite of their difficulties. The research identified that the children who did well had a number of protective factors that helped them to handle their problems. These protective factors included problem-solving ability, the ability to accomplish tasks alone, emotional support from outside the family, the belief that one can influence one's own destiny, and the ability to get on well with others.

To put it simply, they said that a resilient person:

> *"Loves well by having loving caring relationships in their lives, works well by being successful in their job, plays well by having hobbies and enjoying leisure time, and expects a positive future for their lives".*

Werner & Smith's work launched the field of resiliency research, and nowadays studies into resilience continue as we strive to understand and develop strategies that will enable people to become more resilient and how this can help protect us from the stress and strain of modern life.

The reason we need to develop our resilience now, more than ever before, is that not only is the pace of life increasing but so is the amount of stress-related illness. We are spending less time communicating, interacting face to face, and more time communicating via computers and gadgets. Whilst technology is brilliant, nothing is as effective and emotionally rewarding as direct face-to-face contact with other people. This same modern technology has allowed us to be connected to work 24/7 so people are not relaxing and unwinding properly at weekends and evenings. It comes as no surprise then that stress has become the number one reason for people to be off work, on long-term sick leave [*CIPD survey, Nov 2011*].

I believe that by working on developing our resilience, we can ensure that we have the Bounce-back Ability to help us buffer the turbulent effects of the rollercoaster of modern life.

My own research into resilience, highlighted why I felt so frazzled, fragile and worn out. For a variety of reasons the life I had been leading, and my reactions to it, had weakened my resilience. Since that realisation, I have been working on developing my personal resilience and I now feel that I do have the tools in place to enable me to handle the rollercoaster of life more effectively.

This book is the result of my personal journey to increase my own resilience; I call it developing my Bounce-back Ability. I know that my clients have benefited from the tips and advice about resilience that I have been able to give them and I sincerely hope that you will benefit too. It is my hope that you can use the tips and information in this book to help develop your personal resilience.

In each of the chapters, I will share with you a key aspect of my **'Bounce-back Ability Tool Kit'** and I will give you an opportunity to 'Take a Moment for Personal Reflection' where you can focus on relevant areas or issues. At the end of each chapter, I will give you my top tips for ways to develop your own 'Bounce-back Ability'. The 'Bounce-back Ability Tool Kit' comprises the following six **B.O.U.N.C.E.** components, contained within the chapters of this book:

Belief in your ability to cope (See Chapter 1)

Optimism & goals (See Chapters 3 and 4)

s**U**rvival (See Chapter 2)

Nurture (See Chapter 7)

Connection & support (See Chapter 6)

Enjoyment of celebration and gratitude (See Chapter 5)

So make sure you work on all the different areas of B.O.U.N.C.E. and you will keep your Bounce-back Ability in tip-top shape.

Remember, once you have B.O.U.N.C.E., you have your Bounce-back Ability.

As with anything important in life, you reap what you sow. I do urge you to take the time to complete the 'Take a Moment for Personal Reflection' sections. Feel free to write in the space in the book. Or if you don't like writing in books, then keep a notebook handy as you read, so you can jot things down as needed and complete the reflection moments in your book.

It is from these 'Moments for Personal Reflection' that you will develop greater self-awareness and understanding. It is this insight that will empower and enable you to take steps to build your own Bounce-back Ability.

"If you want a better world, first get busy in your own corner"

Anon

Chapter One

Change is a fact of life

> *"When we are no longer able to change a situation, we are challenged to change ourselves."*
> Victor Frankl

No matter how much we may resist it, change is a fact of life. Every part of our world is in a constant state of change, from the cells of our skin to the seasons of nature and the clouds moving across the sky, the world is in a constant state of flux, and change is omnipresent.

There is no doubt though that modern life seems to be moving faster than ever. Technologies are changing the very fabric of our lives, altering forever the way we do everyday tasks, both at work and at home. Family life too has changed over the years as we move away from our roots looking for work and the higher levels of divorce results in scattered families. Fluctuating levels of wealth in global and local economies also brings many changes to our lives such as restructuring at work, cuts to local spending in our communities and the ever-constant squeeze on our budgets. Thus having the ability to handle change and juggle multiple roles is more essential than ever before. Handling change effectively, is an important part of the Bounce-back Ability Tool Kit.

The type of change that is thrust upon us can be difficult to handle. Change is universal and unique, all at the same time. The way we cope with change differs depending upon the situation and each of us reacts differently to change. Some people, for example, cope quite happily with change at work because they view it a natural part of the work environment. However if things in their home life change it throws them into panic and despair. Others can cope with changes in home life but require their work to be routine and rhythmic. Neither reaction is right nor wrong but the fact remains that change in all areas of our lives is inevitable. It has always been part of life's rich tapestry and amazingly, as human beings, we are perfectly able to cope with change.

There are people that naturally embrace change, accepting it, thriving on it and seeing it as part of their own personal growth journey. These people have one of the factors needed for resiliency. The ability to handle change effectively is something that we can all learn to do and the first step is to alter the way we view change.

In order to do that, it may be helpful to understand about the stages that we go through as we adapt and cope, especially when the change has been thrust upon us like divorce, death, redundancy etc.

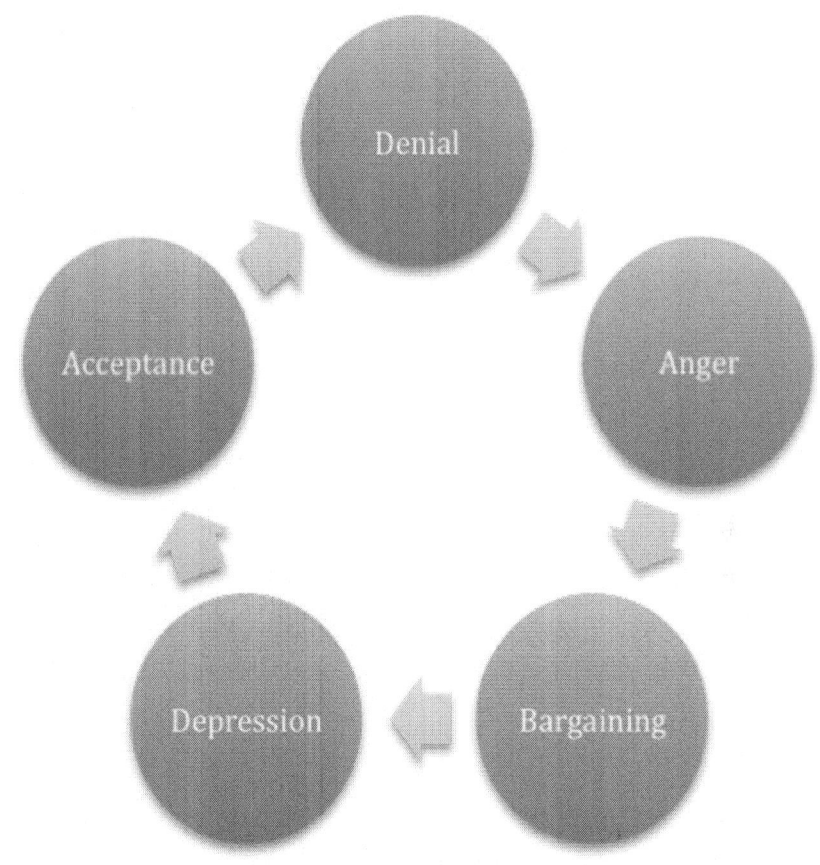

Diagram 1 - Elements of the cycle of change

When we first hear about the change, we can go into **denial** and refuse to accept the facts and reality of the situation. Resistance is normal as you come to terms with the situation.

At some stage, you may experience **anger**. Anger is a natural emotion to feel when change is upon us, whether that anger is directed inward at ourselves or outward at others.

Another stage is **bargaining** which is when you seek to negotiate the terms of the change. For example, when splitting up from a partner, attempts at reconciliation and friendship may be made.

Another powerful emotional stage in the process is **depression and sadness**, which can be acceptance with emotional attachment.

Finally, the last stage is **acceptance** when we can be objective about the situation and more emotionally detached from it.

It is important to note that you can experience these stages in any order.

So how do you handle change?

The following questions are designed to help you reflect on your attitude to change. Once you know how you handle change, both good and not so good, then you can start to take steps to changing the way you think about change. This will then enable you to take steps to change behaviour patterns so that you can grow and become more resilient.

Take a Moment for Personal Reflection Number 1

Stop, and take a moment to reflect on how you view change. Ask yourself the following questions

1. **Do I embrace change?**

2. **Do I accept change?**

3. **Do I thrive on change and see it as part of my personal growth?**

4. **Do I see opportunity within change?**

5. Do I resist change?

6. Do I convince myself it is unnecessary, and refuse to accept it becoming rigid and inflexible, holding tension and stress in my body?

7. Do I partially accept change, but pine for the way things used to be not really moving forward, whilst still having one foot in the past?

Learning point

You may go through all of the above at different times in your life, in response to different changes and your perception of those changes. What is important is that we learn to let go of judgment of what is happening to our life, and us. For when we accept change and choose to embrace it, we empower ourselves.

Take a Moment for Personal Reflection Number 2

Think about the main areas of your life

1. Home
2. Family
3. Work
4. Leisure/ hobbies

On a scale of 1 to 10 (Where 1 is 'I can't cope', and 10 is 'bring it on, I can deal with it') how comfortable are you with change in this area?

Learning point
This reflection will give you increased awareness of the areas of your life in which you are comfortable with change. If scores are low in a particular area (less than 5), please take time to reflect on this and think about what the reason may be. Have you experienced uncomfortable or difficult change in this area on the past? What did you learn from this that can help you be stronger and more resilient? How can you change your perception of change in that area of your life? Even one small change can help reduce anxiety and stress.

Top tips for handling change

1. **Learn any lessons and then let go of the past.** There is nothing to be gained from dwelling on the past because you cannot change it. View your life with more kindness. Stop beating yourself up about things from the past. Instead of moaning and saying, 'what was I thinking?' Take a deep breath and ask the kinder question, 'what was I learning?'

2. **Accept the circumstances that cannot be changed - stop arguing with reality.** Ask yourself, what you are resisting? What are you saying no to, exactly? Be honest with yourself, it is not helpful to lie to yourself; you undermine your self-confidence and cause yourself unnecessary stress.

3. **Acknowledge the part of you that is resisting change**; it is your subconscious mind trying to protect you. Next, simply ask yourself what is its intention; what is it protecting you from? An answer may come straight away, or realisation may come later. You can then 'Thank it' for

keeping you safe and for protecting what is important to you.

4. **Be willing to cope with change**. It may sound very simple but like many things, the simple solutions are the best. By simply changing your attitude and becoming willing to cope, you change your mindset. Be willing to look wider and deeper and see opportunity within the change. Most importantly believe you can cope. Look for evidence in the past that strengthens your belief that you can cope. Recall a time when you have coped well with change. What strengths did you draw on at that time? Remember you are stronger than you realise.

5. **Look for the opportunity within the change**. It is there; you just need to raise your awareness to see it. You need to be willing to be creative in your thinking.

6. **Take control**. There will be parts of the change process that you can control. Recognise what they are and act on what you want to change. Also, recognise those situations that you cannot change; the important point here is to change your attitude to them. Attitude can always be adjusted.

7. **You only have one energy supply, use it wisely**. In other words, don't waste your energy fighting stuff that you do not have control of or cannot influence.

8. **Watch your language**. Are you using the 'victim language' of 'I should', 'I couldn't help it', etc. We all have choices about what we say and how we say it. We all choose how we react to situations.

9. **Express and acknowledge your emotions**. Emotions are a release valve. Feel free to scream (warn family and neighbours first though, so as to prevent any unnecessary 999 calls!). Cry and weep if you need to. If you want to cry but just can't seem to let go, then my tip is to watch a tearjerker movie, get a box of tissues. And for me, as soon as the emotion gets flowing, so do my tears. You may well feel wiped out afterwards but it is important to let go of the emotion and tension in your body. Exercise is another way of burning off or releasing pent up emotions.

10. **How important is this?** Ask yourself will this situation / incident / crisis be important in 5 years' time? If the answer is no, then let it go. If the answer is yes, then trust in your ability to work your way around obstacles.

"When you change the way you look at things, the things you look at change."

Wayne Dyer

Chapter Two

Are you a victim, or survivor?

> *"The price of anything is the amount of life you exchange for it."*
> Henry David Thoreau

We have touched a little already on changing the way we think, in particular about change. I now want you to challenge the most important thought of all about yourself in regard to handling change. Do you see yourself as a victim or a survivor? It is an important question to ask yourself as it impacts on your Bounce-back Ability.

We all go through hard times and we all go through change and upheaval at various points in our lives. This is a fact of life. We have already talked about how we deal with change that feels especially difficult. Equally important though is how we see ourselves during those times. Do you see yourself during those hard times as a victim of circumstances or as a survivor of one of life's twists?

This may not be a question you have asked yourself before, or even really considered. So, how do you tell the difference between victim and survivor mentality?

Take a Moment for Personal Reflection Number 3

Step one is to listen to yourself and the language you use. This applies both to your internal head chatter and the words you use when talking to others about situation X and life in general. So for 1-week make a commitment to yourself to become aware of the language you use. Write down your observations in a notebook or on a piece of paper. Below are some questions to ask yourself to help you reflect on your language.

1. **Do you blame others for your misfortune?**

2. **Do you feel passive and powerless?**

3. **Do you feel life is unfair?**

4. Are you feeling like the world is against you?

5. Do you feel sorry for yourself?

6. Are you looking to others to provide a solution to your situation?

7. Do you feel like you are not in control of your own life?

If the answer to any of the above is yes, then you are indulging in victim mentality.

> **Learning point**
>
> The important point here is to raise your awareness of your language use. Once you have awareness then you can start to make changes to your language patterns. It is possible to change the way you think and speak about situations; it is possible to go from victim to survivor. It doesn't happen overnight but awareness, commitment and practice will help you break that habit.

It may feel rather harsh if, after doing the last personal reflection exercise, you come to the realisation that you are speaking and behaving like a victim. If you have picked up this book because you are currently going through a hard time, the fact that you are thinking like a victim may come as a shock to you. It certainly did to me when I came to that realisation. You may well even feel like throwing the book down in disgust. Don't do it! Stay with me and continue to read, learn, and change your life for the better.

It is amazing, but you do have the enormous power and potential to change your own life. In fact, the reality is that you are the only person who can. And I speak from experience, as I have personally moved from victim mentality to survivor mentality. One very simple change you can make is to change your attitude to a situation. This will give you control and you can then start to shift from victim to survivor.

Trust me, I know from experience, what a difference your attitude to a situation can make. I haven't always had the best attitude and I have had my moments of feeling like a victim. I'm not saying that it's not all right to have a few moments of self-pity and tears, especially when the situation is fresh and emotions are strong. It is important to feel the emotion and let it out. Burying emotion deep within us is not a good habit. The key I have found, is to feel it, let it out, then move on mentally and allow yourself to heal. Long term, an attitude of self-pity, blame (both others and ourselves) and frequent tears is not going to help. Thinking as a victim is disempowering and makes you more vulnerable and less resilient.

At this point in time it is vital not to dwell on thinking, 'Why am I thinking like a victim?'. Do not beat yourself up about it mentally. Simply acknowledge the realisation of your victim mentality and then make a decision to change. For the purpose of building resilience, the key here is to simply decide to become a survivor.

The next step to building resilience is to change your thinking in relation to 'Situation X', whatever that situation may be. Try looking at the situation from a different angle.

An excellent way to do this is to put yourself in the other person's position. How might they behave in your situation? To do this, simply close your eyes and imagine seeing, hearing, and feeling their reactions to Situation X. Set aside your own feeling and beliefs about Situation X. Replay Situation X from the other person viewpoint. Imagine you are stepping right into their shoes. Now look through their eyes and see what they see. Listen through their ears, hear what they hear, and then imagine you are in their body so you can feel what they feel.

- What insights to seeing the situation differently did you gain?

- What can you learn from this?

- Even one small insight can give you a new perspective that can help.

Take this one new insight and use it to help you change the way you view your situation. This will help to move you from victim to survivor. Build on this, one step at a time. Start to find ways to lessen your victim mentality in other areas of your life as well. It may take time but better to be moving slowly towards being a survivor than to stay a victim.

If you feel that you need to know why you have had a victim mentality in the past then I recommend you get yourself a good counsellor. Find someone suitably qualified who can support you on the journey.

A good resource is the British Association for Counselling and Psychotherapy http://www.bacp.co.uk

The next step to being a resilient survivor is changing your attitude and beliefs about blame. Do you blame yourself or do you blame others?

Blame is the easy option. It passes responsibility to others. Blame also means others are responsible for your happiness. They have the control over your life. Is that really how you want to live? This realisation was a big wake up call for me especially in regard to relationship breakdowns.

In reality, each of us is responsible for our own actions and our own part in every aspect of our lives as adults. Remember it is all right to make mistakes; we are, after all, human beings and not machines. What is essential is that you learn from those mistakes and in time, they can become part of your success story.

When you accept responsibility for your wrong turns in life, you can also accept credit for your correct turns and good decisions. Accepting responsibility is very powerful it gives you control over your happiness and your own destiny.

Learning to live in the moment of now, by not dwelling in the past is part of building your resilient skills.

Once you have stopped blaming others it is then important to stop creating obstacles and excuses. When you have done this, then it becomes possible to start channelling your energy into finding solutions and taking proactive decisions.

Remember you are only a victim if you allow yourself to be one.

> *"Self-pity is easily the most destructive of non-pharmaceutical narcotics; it is addictive, gives momentary pleasure and separates the victim from reality."*
> John W Gardner

Let us now focus on the survivor mentality and how having this attitude makes such a difference to your Bounce-back Ability.

The difference is that people with a survivor mentality take charge of the situation and find solutions that work for them.

Survivors assess the situation, control their reactions and create solutions.

They say, "OK, this situation is happening; now I need to find a solution".

It is impossible for us to control other people and their behaviours. It is possible to control our own reactions and attitudes to those people and situations. This gives you control and power over your own life. If your happiness depends on changing others then you have no power.

Individuals with a survivor mentality not only take control of whatever they can in a situation, they also make the most of what they can't control by adjusting their attitude to it. This attitude gives them flexibility of mind which is what actually then gives them control over the outcome of the situation and helps them to remain positive and focused on what is right for them.

Sometimes people with a survivor mentality also have a bit of a 'gallows sense of humour' that kicks in during particularly dramatic situations. This is something I do; I have found it helps me to cope. Gallows humour allows you to make light of your difficulties and use humour as a release valve. This has the effect of lightening the load mentally and can be very beneficial. Plus when we laugh, we release feel-good chemicals, which help us to heal physically as well as mentally. Having said that, it is important to note that, not everyone around us may understand why we are behaving like this. One has to be careful not to offend others. I personally find my gallows sense of humour is a great coping mechanism and is very much part of my Bounce-back Ability Tool Kit.

The language we use can help to identify whether we are victim or survivor. There are several well-known phrases that you hear people saying in relation to a survivor mentality such as "God / The Universe never gives you more than you can handle", "That which doesn't kill us, makes us stronger", and my favourite:

> *"Women are like teabags, we don't know our true strength until we are in hot water."*
> *Eleanor Roosevelt.*

In order to start to speak more like a survivor it is important to start to use language that is more positive. This will help you become more optimistic in your outlook. The first step is to pause and think before speaking. In many cases, we open our mouth and the words fall out before we have really thought about them. Many of our speech patterns are habitual. The good news is a habit can be changed. It just takes a decision to do it, awareness of when we do it, then a commitment to change.

The next step in the process is the all-important practice, practice, and more practice. Raise your awareness of the language patterns of your friends and family. Are they using negative victim language? Beware it can be toxic and can drag you down mentally.

Are you worried about what others will think of you pausing and being slower to respond? Rest assured it is all right to pause before you speak. In fact, in some cultures it is considered polite.

An important step is to censor yourself so that when you catch yourself using negative words and phrases, you stop mid-sentence and reframe more positively. Friends and family may ask you why you are doing this; just tell them you are learning to develop a more positive outlook. People will be intrigued and may even want to join in, which is great. The more positive thinkers and speakers the better we will all feel.

Finally, commit to being conscious and conscientious about your language. By focusing on what you want, not what you don't want, you give yourself more power to live life your way.

An example of a subtle change in language is:

> *"I won't let X have a detrimental effect on my life."*

This can be made even better by rephrasing to:

> *"The effect on my life of X is minimal."*

Similarly:

> *"I didn't do that"*

Now becomes:

> *"What I actually did was…"*

Try it, and get friends to join in. It can be fun and it will help you become aware of the language your friends use too.

Top tips for developing a survivor mindset

1. **Choose to have a survivor mindset**. This starts with just saying to yourself that you are a survivor. Tell yourself that you will find ways to improvise to adapt. Tell yourself you will overcome adversity. To succeed we must first believe we can.

2. **Watch your language**. Eliminate negative and blame words such as, **"but, it's not my fault"** from your language. Other examples are, "I was forced to" becomes, "I will choose to" and, "it will never work" becomes, "Let us try and find another way". Remember your body language too. How do you walk, sit and stand? Unmotivated people, and people with victim mentality, tend to walk looking down at the ground, shoulders slumped, and they move and talk very slowly. Confident focused people look up more; they talk with more energy and animation in their voice and their posture is firmer and stronger. Stand with your shoulders back and your head held high to help to change your physiology. Acting like a survivor helps you think and behave like one to.

3. **Accept responsibility**, it's your life. Instead of giving yourself reasons why you can't do something, give yourself reasons why you can. This is far more powerful and empowering.

4. **Find solutions**. Remember, survivors are solution-finders. Tell yourself you can do it. It does not all have to be done at once either; to start with, you just need to take that first step. What one step can you take today that will make you a survivor?

5. **Get to know and understand yourself better**. What are your strengths and weaknesses? What are your beliefs? A belief is simply something that you hold to be true. We can hold beliefs about ourselves that empower us and beliefs that limit us. Recognising your limiting beliefs and working to overcome them is very beneficial part of personal growth and development. If you do not know what your beliefs about yourself are, you may find it helpful to work through those with a professional life coach. No man is an island; we all need support and help. This help can come from friends and family but they are intimately involved in your life so may try to influence you. A coach is not there to judge or influence and is not intimately

involved in your life, so they can be impartial and support you in finding your solution. Where you need to unpick deeper concerns then seek help from a professional therapist. It is important to understand how your values and beliefs affect your life choices. I personally have used a number of different tools to help me challenge my limiting beliefs, change my thinking and implement new behaviours. I have used both counselling and coaching to help me at different points on my journey. I have learnt a lot about myself along the way and found solutions that work for me. The most important point is that I know that I am a survivor, and so are you.

6. **Forgive yourself**. Do not dwell on mistakes. Learn the lesson, forgive yourself and the other person / people, and move on. If you harbour anger and hurt, then you do not allow yourself to heal. This can be destructive and disempowering. There are a number of ways to forgive yourself. One I have found very helpful is to write a letter. This can be to yourself, to the person who you feel has wronged you or to an imaginary person. Simply start writing and let it flow. I pour it all out on paper and then when I have no more to say I ask for forgiveness of myself. Then I have a

ceremonial burning of the letter. As the letter goes up in flames, I say aloud that I forgive myself and the other person / people. I thank them for the lessons that I have learnt and I give myself permission to forgive them and myself. Then I give myself permission to move on with my life. This simple ceremony allows me to vent my emotions, then release and forgive. I take with me the learning and the wisdom and leave the rest in the past.

7. **Be your own best friend** and talk nicely to yourself. Do you have a little voice in your head? If your internal head chatter is saying something about yourself that you would not say aloud about your best friend, looking her / him directly in the eye, then why are you saying this type of stuff to yourself? Negative head-chatter undermines you and prevents you moving forward. Start learning to be kinder to yourself and say nicer things to yourself.

8. **Manage your moods**. Managing your moods is very important, but something people seldom think about. In fact, some people think they can't control their moods. The truth of course is that we can. But, like everything, it needs to be learnt and

practiced. By managing your mood, you will be able to make better decisions. Here are a few tips to help you get started. Set the intention in the morning that today is going to be a great day. Some people find positive statements, that they read out each morning, to be beneficial. Others find inspiring pictures, music, or motivation tapes help. I, personally, take a few moments each morning to look through my motivational quotes, then 'Tweet it' and 'Post it to my Facebook page'. This really helps me. A lovely knock on effect is that my friends have also commented on how much it helps them too, which is brilliant. I also have one of my goal maps [Mayne] pinned on the wall of my bathroom. Looking at that each morning, helps me focus on my plans and my future. If something happens during the day to knock you off balance and make you sad / angry / fed up, be aware that you are allowing something external to control you. Allow yourself a bit of time to refocus, take a deep breath, go for a walk around the block, then choose to get back into a calmer more positive mood. Again, keep the faith and remember that practice makes for improvement.

9. **Change your focus**. Focus on what you want not what you don't want. So for example, if you are separated / divorced and you don't want an argument with your ex when s/he picks the kids up, focus on developing more constructive positive interactions with her/him. So instead of thinking, 'I don't want another argument with her/him today." say to yourself, "Today I am going to be tolerant and find ways to improve things for my children". It will help your kids too, to see you focused on positivity. This is one that I have used to help me, and I am proud of the excellent relationship that I have developed with the father of my children. It hasn't always been easy and at times has taken a lot of emotional effort, but my reward is that my kids have thrived, despite divorce.

10. **Make a note of your language**. Buy a nice notebook; keep it by your bed and each night write down an example of words you have used that you wish you had said more positively. Write down what you said, and then rewrite it as you wish you had said it. Slowly but surely, you will start to notice that you need to do this less and less as your language becomes more survivor-type and less victim-type.

"If it's never our fault, we can't take responsibility for it. If we can't take responsibility for it, we will always be its victim."

Richard Bach

Chapter Three

The future is bright, the future is yours!

> *"Your future is created by what you do today, not tomorrow."*
> *Robert Kiyosaki*

Believing that your outlook is hopeful, i.e. being optimistic, is a key part of developing resilience. I am not suggesting that you ignore the issues and the problems that you are facing and pretend everything in the world is rosy. Putting your fingers in your ears, closing your eyes and humming loudly to ignore the situation is a comical, not practical solution. This type of behaviour is blind optimism. This is actually a way of refusing to face reality, of not taking control of your life and being a victim. Remember we talked about the victim mentality in the previous chapter.

What I am talking about here is being a genuine optimist. As I have said this does not mean ignoring problems, it is in fact quite the opposite. Being a genuine optimist means assessing the problem or situation, knowing that it is part of the ups and downs of life. Then, having faith in your own ability to find a solution that is right for you. Finally, know that you can, and will, implement that solution and adjust to a new way. The essence here is simply believing, "That whatever happens, I will be OK".

It is important to learn to trust in yourself and your problem-solving abilities. Know that the solutions you are working on will be taking you towards being in a better and brighter place mentally, spiritually and physically.

You may be asking, "Where do these solutions come from?" They come from you. You can ask others how they might handle the situation, so that you can examine different options available, but the reality is that the most successful solutions to your situation are the ones you create.

Take a Moment for Personal Reflection Number 4

Take a sheet of paper and write down the essence of a current problem or situation that is challenging you.

Now write down a list of potential ways that you can solve the problem or rectify the situation. Put down everything that you can think of, even things for which you do not currently have the resources or skills.

When I do this, I treat it like a brainstorming exercise and scribble it all down. I put the problem in the centre of the page and draw a circle around it then, as I think up solutions, I add them around the edge and connect them to the problem by a line.

From this brainstorming, work out which of the ideas is the simplest to implement and the most likely to get you started on the path to solving or changing your problem or situation.

Focus on what you want, not what you don't want.

Next, make a commitment to yourself to take that first step.

Set a date you intend to do it by, and then do it. You can always ask a friend to support you, but remember they can't do it for you.

The two roles are: a) that you carry out the action, and b) your friend will provide support, encouragement, and will hold you accountable if you do not complete it. This ensures that you deliver on your promise to yourself to take action. Remember part of being resilient is to understand that you must accomplish things yourself and that you shape your own future, supported by your friends and family.

> **Learning Point**
>
> Hard as it may be, it is vital that you find the solutions. They are more likely to be successful if they are your choices and your actions. By all means, bounce ideas off friends and family, but you need to decide what is right for you. If you need more formalised help then a good professional coach can support you on this part of your journey.

Remember to take things one-step at a time. It makes things simpler, less overwhelming and more manageable. After all, you have nothing to lose by trying and everything to gain. If your solution does not work out, just look for the lesson you need to learn. Understand it, and accept that setbacks are part of life and are only temporary. Then try another way. Remind yourself that you are strong, that you are capable and that you are resilient. Things do not always work first time. Find the learning point and try again. Remember there is no such thing as failure only feedback.

By doing this you will learn to let go of your fears and trust in your abilities and yourself. You are the most reliable, dependable source of solutions for your personal situation.

Maintaining a hopeful outlook may seem like a huge hurdle to overcome but it is key to building resilience. For me there have been times in the past when I have struggled to maintain a hopeful outlook. Wherever I looked, I seemed to see trouble and strife. There have been times when I have been trapped in a cycle of negative thoughts and worries, just like the diagram below.

Round and round, in circles of negative thinking I would go.

Diagram 2 - Negative Thinking

Then in 2010, I attended an excellent workshop run by Brian Mayne, called Goal Mapping for Success. He explained in very simple terms the brain chemistry of negative and positive thinking.

To put it simply when you think negatively, you release Coritsol (one of our stress hormones), and this 'shuts down' your brain, halting the brain cell connections. Thus trapping you in a cycle of negative thought.

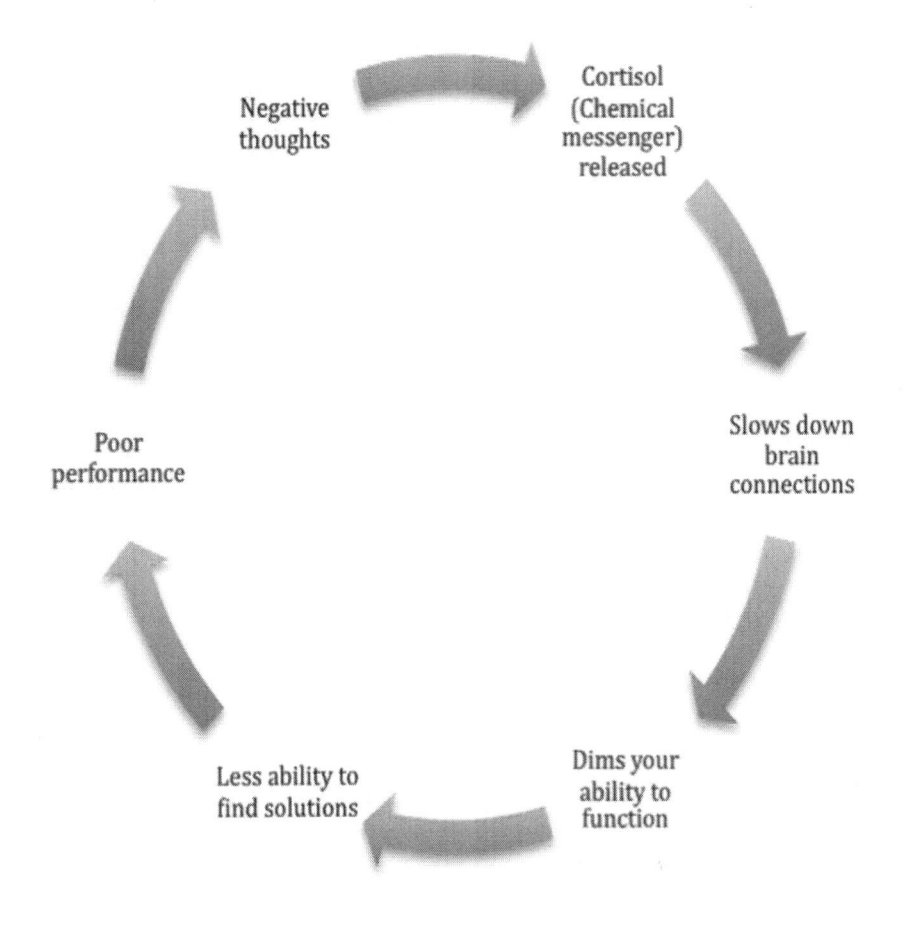

Diagram 3 - Negative Thought Cycle

So the first step to believing your outlook is hopeful, is to change the way you think.

Conversely, when you think positively, you release Serotonin (a feel good hormone) in the brain, which 'lights' your brain up, stimulating lots of brain cell connections and encouraging the flow of thoughts.

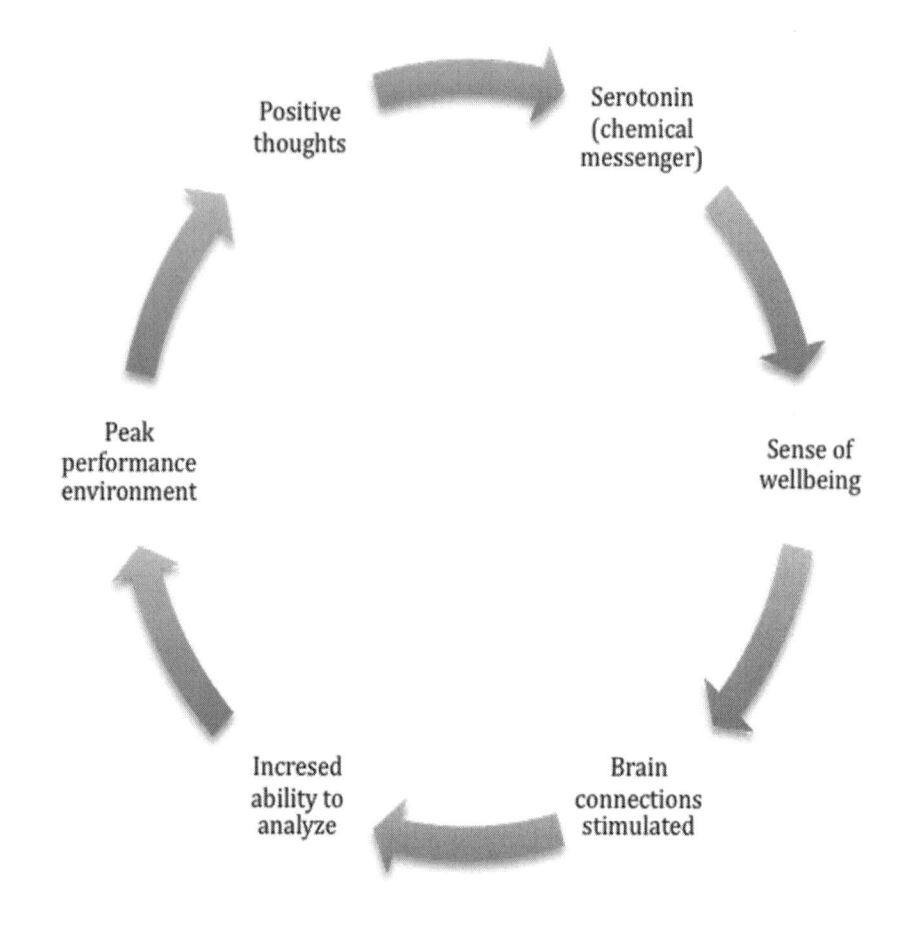

Positive thoughts → Serotonin (chemical messenger) → Sense of wellbeing → Brain connections stimulated → Incresed ability to analyze → Peak performance environment → (back to Positive thoughts)

Diagram 4 - Positive Thought Cycle

Learning this simple information, that is backed by neuroscience research, was a light-bulb moment for me. I started working on changing my thinking. It didn't happen overnight, as I was well-practiced at negative thinking, to the point where it was a habitual mindset. However, the good news is that habits can be broken and replaced with new ones. The important thing to remember is that it does not just happen instantly. It takes practice, practice, and more practice. The key here is the decision to change your thinking and then the commitment to do it, combined with the belief that you can do it. Essentially, whenever I found myself thinking negatively, I paused and rephrased it using more positive words. For example, simply changing, 'I can't do this' to, 'I can't do this, yet' changes the meaning; taking it from a negative dead end statement to introducing the element of possibility and personal growth. Another example is when I heard myself saying, "I have a problem at work" I changed it to "I have a situation at work that I am working on resolving".

The reason changing the way you think is so important to developing resilience is because your thoughts, feelings and behaviours are all interlinked.

You have a thought, which leads to a feeling; this in turn, leads to you taking an action. Such a process forms our behaviour.

THOUGHT

FEELING

BEHAVIOUR

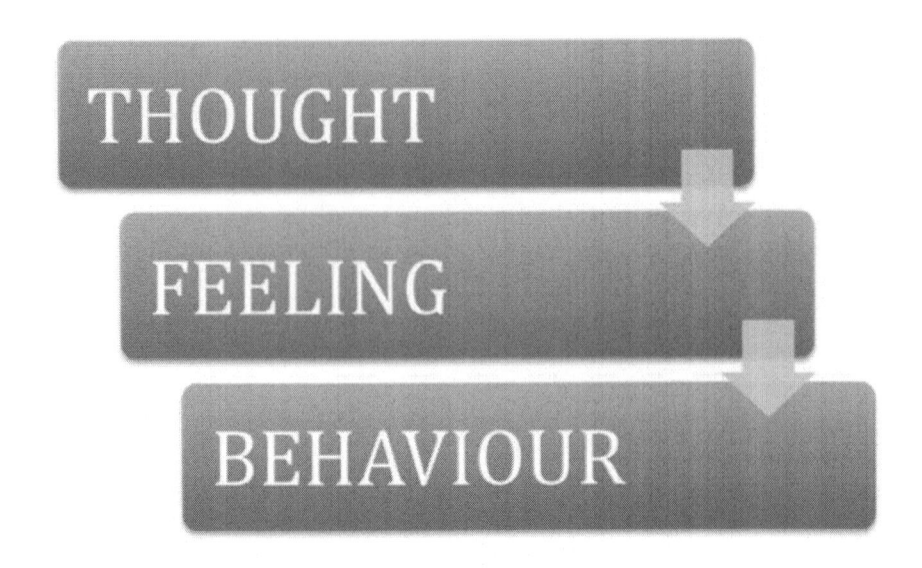

Diagram 5 - Thought Feeling Behaviour

So in order to develop resilient behaviours you first need to change the way you think and be more optimistic about your future.

Top tips for developing a hopeful outlook

1. **Pause, before you label a situation or event negative or positive**. Life is a rich tapestry full of lots of different experiences. From everything, we can learn a lesson that will allow us to grow and develop as a person. Sometimes life gives us what we want and sometimes it gives us what we need to grow and develop.

2. **Watch your language** both for your internal head-chatter and your external normal talking. If you catch yourself thinking negatively, or speaking negatively, then 'Flip It'. You can get more help and inspiration from Michael Heppell's book, '*Flip It*'. I thoroughly recommend reading this if you are struggling with habitual negative thinking. An example of Flip It is:

    'I'm tired' (**Flip It**) 'I could use a bit more energy.'

    'I haven't got time' (**Flip It**) 'How can I make time?'

3. **Learn to manage your emotions**. Emotions are like waves to a surfer, you can't stop them but you can choose which ones you want to ride. Neuroscience research has shown that it is possible to manage our emotional responses.

Take anger for example. In theory any associated chemicals released by your body when you trigger the anger will dissipate within 90seconds. Therefore, if you remain angry it is because you are choosing to. This means the anger circuit remains running releasing more stress chemicals. The advice is to become aware of your physical triggers (notice if you are clenching your jaw, fist, breathing fast and shallow) then take two or three deep breaths, breathing out more slowly than you breathed in. Acknowledge the emotion, and then reframe it into a more positive response. It takes practice but it does work. Remember, practice makes for improvement. If this is a sticking point for you then get professional help to support you in your desire to change. Anger management classes or Cognitive Behavioural Therapy (CBT) is particularly good.

4. **Play the hero in your own life story**. Many people dream of a knight in shining armour that rides in and saves them. The reality is that you are the only person who can actually make those heroic moves. You can get help and support on your journey, but you have to take the first heroic step. Have faith in your own ability.

5. **You are what you eat, so feed your brain properly**. Eating a balanced diet is essential for healthy living and the usual rule of five portions of fruit and vegetables, eight glasses of non-caffeine fluids goes without saying. But there are also a couple of key nutrition elements that help you to be more positive and focused. Firstly, maintain balanced blood sugar levels. The brain needs a constant supply of blood sugar in order to work effectively. Both too much, and too little, sugar causes problems that affect your moods, attention and memory. Eating refined sugars (white bread, white pasta, and white rice) and drinking sugar-laden drinks is not good for the brain. Eating carbohydrates that release their sugars slowly such as wholegrain wheat, brown pasta, brown rice, sweet potatoes, and oats provides a more stable blood sugar level for the brain. Next, ensure your diet is rich in the good guys of the fat world, Omega 3. You find this naturally in oily fish and some nuts and seeds. Research has shown that in some patients, Omega 3 supplements can be as effective as anti-depressants in managing mild depression. If you have any doubt about your diet, keep a food diary for a week. This will raise your awareness of what you are eating and any poor

habits you have developed. You can then consult a nutritionist to give you advice on ways to improve it if you wish. Taking a fish oil supplement is good but ensure that it is of clinical grade level like PuraEPA.

6. **Fake it, until you make it**. Your brain cannot differentiate between situations you are thinking about and things that are happening. So when you think about something the brain fires up as if you are actually doing it. This is called positive pre-play and is used a lot by successful sports people to improve performance. Essentially, if you visualise yourself coping and see yourself having a positive future you will strengthen the brain connections. This means that if you imagine yourself doing something successfully before you actually take that first step you make it easier to achieve. You have primed yourself for peak performance.

"Every situation is a positive situation if I view it as an opportunity for growth and self-mastery."

Brian Tracey

Chapter Four

Take one step at a time towards your goals

> *"Without goals and plans to reach them, you are like a ship that sets sail with no destination."*
> *Fitzhugh Dodson*

The next step to developing resilience is developing realistic goals and then taking decisive steps to move towards them. In earlier chapters, we looked briefly at how survivors find solutions. Now it is time to take those solutions and turn them into step-by-step goals.

There are a couple of points that I feel are important to make here. The first is that, when the rollercoaster of life has thrown you into a dip, this does not mean that you cannot achieve your big life goals. You may just need to be a little more flexible and creative in the steps that you take to get there. You may need to alter your timelines to achieve them, giving yourself more time and flexibility. But if you really want that particular goal, it is still achievable. Ask yourself if it is what you really truly desire, and if you feel like it is part of your purpose in life, your destiny. Secondly, you may decide that, in light of the lessons you have learnt from this particular dip on the rollercoaster, that one goal that you previously aspired to no longer feels right. This is OK. It is your life, so you decide what is right for you and what is important. Remember to accept that circumstances change. As the theologian, Reinhold Niebuhr said:

> *"Grant me the serenity to accept the things that cannot be changed, courage to change the things that I can, and wisdom to know the difference."*
> *Reinhold Niebuhr*

We all achieve goals every day, lots of small ones, without even really thinking about them. If you have ever made a 'To Do List' and then worked through those actions one by one, then you have achieved goals. Even babies achieve goals; you only have to watch a baby learning to walk to know that determination and practice is a powerful combination for success.

Have you experienced times when some actions just seem to stay on the To Do List? These items at the end of each day get moved onto the next day. Do you only complete those items when they reach the point you can no longer avoid them? The reason this usually happens is because those particular items are challenging and move you out of your comfort zone. You avoid them until the time limit or crisis point has been reached and you absolutely have to do them. In those situations, you will have wasted time and valuable energy avoiding them. It is far better to always do the least desired item on your list first. Tough, but true. There is an old saying that if you eat a live frog in the morning, nothing worse can happen for the rest of the day. Brian Tracey wrote a book on overcoming procrastination called 'Eat that Frog' using this saying as inspiration. The idea, very simply, is that your frog is represented by the most difficult item on your to do list. The one you will procrastinate over. If you avoid this item, it will drain you of energy. However, if you do the most difficult item first, it will give you energy and momentum for the rest of the day.

William James, a psychologist said:

> *"Procrastination is attitudes natural assassin. There is nothing as fatiguing as an uncompleted task."*
> *William James*

Remember, you will grow and develop greater resilience as you take decisive action and push yourself out of your comfort zone, one small step at a time. If you feel you need help and support then do not be afraid to ask for it. Remember that professional help can be sort to support you, and to hold your hand on the journey to a more resilient you. You obviously still have to do the hard, but rewarding work, of overcoming your limiting beliefs and the obstacles in your path. But oh, how amazing you will feel when you do it.

Whether you are a seasoned goal setter, or new to it, there is huge value in reflecting on your past achievements and gaining insight into your strengths and weaknesses from goals you have already achieved in life so far.

Take a Moment for Personal Reflection Number 5

When you are building your goal-setting skills it is good to take a moment to reflect on what you have already achieved. This will give you insight; allow you to draw strength from your achievements and remind you what you are capable of.

Ask yourself the following questions:

1. **What have you already achieved so far, in your life?**

2. **What do you consider to be your greatest achievement?**

3. **When did you achieve that?**

4. What obstacles did you have to overcome to achieve it?

5. How did you overcome those obstacles?

6. What, if any, mistakes did you make along the way

7. What was your main reason for achieving this goal?

8. Who helped, influenced and inspired you to achieve?

> **Learning Point**
>
> Reflect upon your past achievements, however big or small. Each is significant in its own way. Have you become aware of any particular strengths or weaknesses?
>
> How can you apply this insight to your current situation?
>
> If you struggled with this, then maybe you are being too hard on yourself or feeling rather low. Come back to it later or seek professional support whilst doing it. I found it hard to do the first time because I was being really negative in my thinking. I came back to it after working on my negative thinking with my coach and it was much easier. In fact, once I started on the small achievements, it was amazing how the bigger ones came back into my mind.

There are two main types of goals short-term and long-term. Short-term goals are steps you need to take that are usually achieved within one day to six months. Long-term goals are those you wish to achieve within a time frame from six months, to any number of years ahead. Short-term goals can simply be items on your To Do List, or they can be a step on the path to your long-term goals.

If your long-term goals are aligned to your purpose in life then, not only are you more likely to achieve them, but you will also have more fun along the way. Some people, such as athletes and artists know early in their life what their purpose is. For others it can be more difficult to define. The reason it is important to identify your purpose is that without it, you can find yourself meandering through life never really feeling connected and in tune with life.

Your purpose is your 'reason why', your reason for living. Purpose is influenced by values and beliefs and is deeply rooted in a person; it gives reason to our actions. When we are aligned with our purpose, it is possible to deal with whatever life is throwing into our path. A strong sense of purpose helps you stay on track to achieve your goals because you are aligned with what your life was meant to be. Purpose helps you to be persistent and resilient enough to deal with the tough bits of life, the rollercoaster dips.

For some of you, this may be the first time you have even thought about what your purpose is. Finding your purpose is a fun and inspiring exercise in developing your self-awareness. It is part of the journey of self-discovery that helps develop your resilience. After all, it is easier to bounce back from a downward dip on the rollercoaster of life if you know you what your purpose is.

It is important clarify the difference between purpose, vision, and goals, as this will help you understand who you truly are. Then your goals will help you accomplish what you were meant to do in life.

Purpose is the reason why you are doing what you choose to do. Vision is what you are doing with your life, and goals are what you set out to do, so that you will take the steps to achieving it.

To find your purpose you must first identify what is important to you and find ways to express this in your life. If you ask yourself, what you can contribute to make the world a better place, then this is a great place to start to find your purpose.

Take a Moment for Personal Reflection Number 6

This is a neat little exercise to start you thinking about what you value in life. It will start you on the path of self-discovery to find your purpose.

Take yourself forward in time to the morning of your 90th birthday. You are blissful and happy. Look back on all you have accomplished in life, your successes, and relationships with friends and family. What matters most to you? What are you most proud of? How did you make your world a better place?

Now write down the answers on the next page.

All about my 90th birthday

All about my 90th birthday (Ctd.)

> **Learning Point**
>
> The purpose of this exercise is to get you to focus on the person you really want to be and the life you want to have led. This can help you to readjust your priorities.

Learning how to set goals and then taking the necessary steps to achieve them is a topic worthy of a whole book. There are lots of goal-setting programmes and books out there. Just type 'tips for goal achieving' into a search engine on the internet and you will get twelve million, eight hundred, possibilities returned.

I personally use a technique called Goal Mapping. I am a qualified 'Brain Mayne, Goal Mapping Practitioner', and I run workshops on the Goal Mapping programme. I like this, because its principles are simple and inspiring. It is a very visual way of setting goals, which strengthens them and optimises you for success.

Come along to one of my workshops, if you want to find out more:

www.helenturier.co.uk

And do check out the Goal Mapping website for more information on courses in your area.

http://www.liftinternational.com

Of course, you are free to choose whatever you wish to support you in your goal setting.

Below, is one of my personal goal maps.

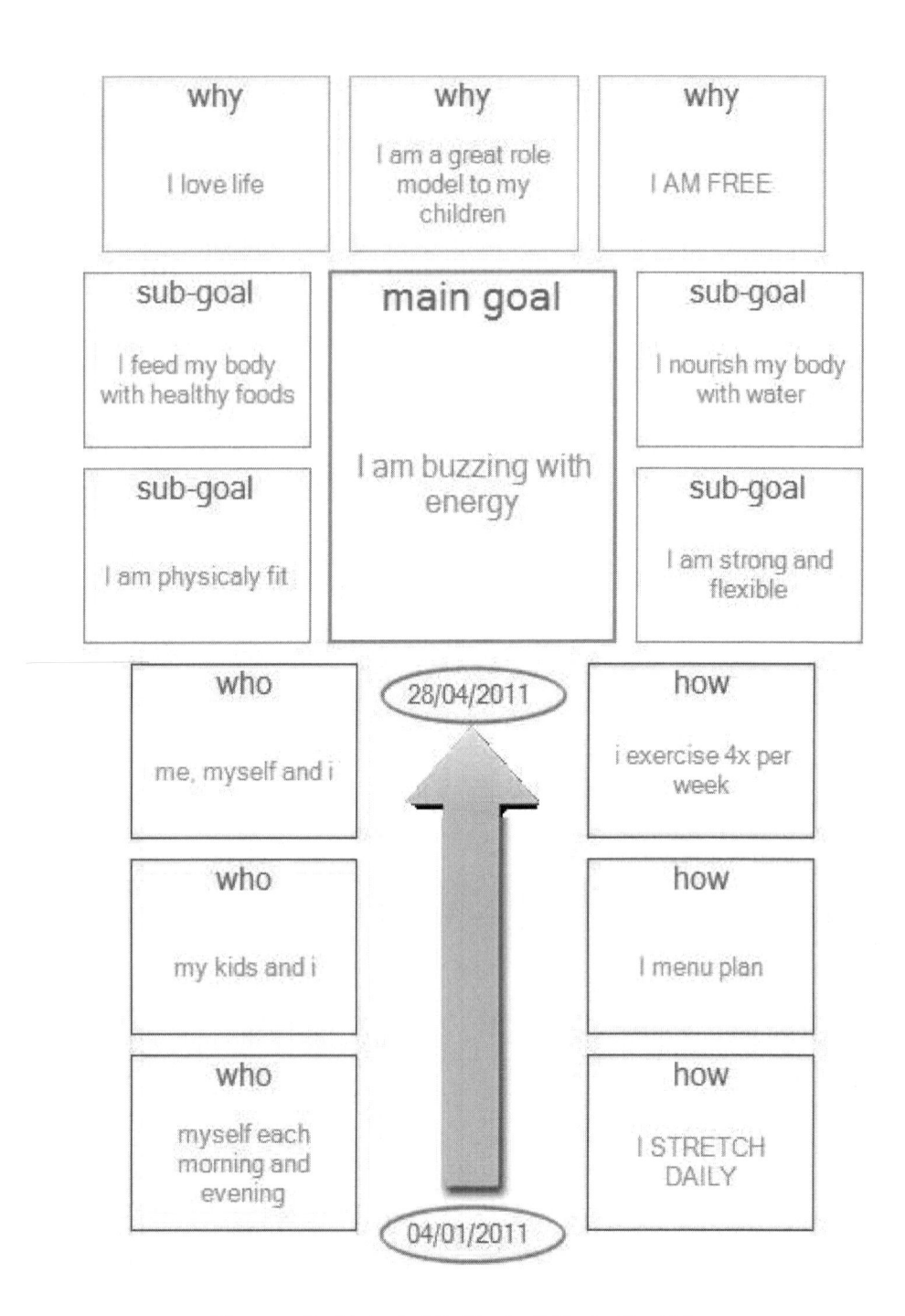

why I love life	why I am a great role model to my children	why I AM FREE

sub-goal I feed my body with healthy foods	main goal I am buzzing with energy	sub-goal I nourish my body with water
sub-goal I am physicaly fit		sub-goal I am strong and flexible

28/04/2011

who me, myself and i	how i exercise 4x per week
who my kids and i	how I menu plan
who myself each morning and evening	how I STRETCH DAILY

04/01/2011

Diagram 6 - Helen's Vitality: Left Brain Goal Map

Diagram 7 - Helen's Vitality: Right Brain Goal Map

Take one step at a time towards your goals - 89

The words are on the left, because the left side of our brain connects more readily with words. And the pictures are on the right, because the right side of the brain is the visual side.

This is a goal map that I created to help me maintain my energy levels through the first quarter of last year. I have found in the past that my energy levels are low at this time of the year. By creating a goal map, focussed around 'buzzing with energy' and then putting it up on my bathroom wall, I was able to focus on it at the start of each day. Doing this each morning helped me to stay committed to my exercise and healthy eating plan.

The main goal is in the centre, with sub-goals on either side. The '**Whys**', at the top of the picture, are my key emotional drivers. If we have a strong 'reason why', it makes goals easier to achieve and we are more committed to succeed. The '**Hows**', are three key steps I can take towards achieving my goal, of course more could be added. The '**Who**', are people who can help you achieve your goals.

Obviously, my kids are an important part of my menu planning, as we eat together at the start and end of each day, so they were my 'who'. Of course, I am the one who has to do the exercise, which is why I am my 'who'; I might also have put down the teacher for my weekly ballet class or the instructor at the gym. The reality though, is it is me who has to actually do the exercise!

Top tips for working towards your goals

1. **One small step at a time**. Break tasks and big goals into bite sized pieces. Then take that first step. Remember you are the only one that can take the first step. It may be hard to do but without taking that first step nothing can change and you will remain where you are. So go on, I know you can do it.

2. **SMART goals**. It's a timeless classic but makes so much sense. Make sure your goals are specific (know what it is you want and pay attention to the detail, that's your baby steps), measureable (assess your progress), achievable (do you believe you can do it?) and relevant (is your goal aligned to your purpose) and timely (be realistic about timeframes).

3. **Get to know yourself**. Finding out more about yourself is a great way to accelerate your Bounce-back Ability. Spend some time listing what makes you smile, what you feel passionately about, what you are good at, and thinking about what you would do if success were guaranteed. These are all great questions to ask yourself. Know your strengths, acknowledge your weaknesses and

commit to taking steps to work on overcoming those weaknesses. This is an excellent way to help move you towards your goals.

4. **The 3 P's**. When you think about your goal and you write it down state it in the **present tense**, using **positive language** and make sure its **personal**. i.e. I have Bounce-back Ability. This is how you set a goal for wanting to achieve better resilience.

5. **Excuses**. You are responsible for your own success. So don't turn excuses into perfectly justified reasons for not doing something. What is stopping you taking that step towards your goal? If you are struggling with something, stop, look and listen. What are you saying to yourself, do you really want to move forward in your life or would you rather stay still? The choice is yours. Look at times you have struggled before, what did you do to overcome the difficulty? Drawing on inspiration from your past successes is a useful way to help yourself move forwards if you get stuck.

6. **Visualise yourself achieving your goals**. Mental practice can help get you closer to achieving what you want. The brain cannot distinguish between imagining and actually doing. Research has

shown that mental rehearsal is hugely beneficial in performance improvement. So imagine yourself achieving your goal, use all your senses to help build the mental picture. See yourself, feel yourself, hear yourself and taste that success. World Champion Golfer, Jack Nicklaus said: "I never hit a shot, not even in practice, without having a very sharp in-focus picture of it in my head".

7. **Use Inspiring Images to help stimulate your brain for success**. Making a mood board of the things that you want in life can help to align you with your purpose and stimulate your brain for success. It's a fun exercise to do. You simply cut out pictures and images from magazines and newspapers, etc. of images that represent the goals you want to achieve. Better still have a go yourself at drawing your images. Then put your finished work of art somewhere you can see it. It will help inspire and motivate you for success in your life.

8. **Get help if you need it**. No man is an island and we all need a little helping hand at times to keep us moving forward. So if you are struggling with making progress then ask for help. It can be as

simple as getting a friend to assist you or having a coaching session with a life coach. You may even want to look at why you are stuck by seeking help from a counsellor. The important thing here is to do something.

9. **Keep track of your progress**. When the pace of life is so fast and, especially if lots of change is happening, it is common to lose sight of your progress. Respect and honour the progress you have made no matter the size of the achievement. Some people keep track by writing a journal. I keep a notebook by the bed and list my 3 positives for each day before I go to sleep at night. That way I keep track of the big things and the little things along the way. I even made myself write in my journal on the day my best friend died. I am not going to share that entry as it is personal but I just wanted you to know that even on the most awful day it is possible to find some positives.

10. **Want to know more about goals and goal-setting? Then come along to a Goal Mapping workshop**.

    www.helenturier.co.uk | www.liftinternational.com

Take one step at a time towards your goals - 95

"You measure the size of the accomplishment by the obstacles you had to overcome to reach your goals."

Booker T Washington

Chapter Five

Celebrate your successes and nurture an attitude of gratitude

> *"Gratitude makes sense of our past, brings peace for today, and creates a vision for tomorrow."*
> *Melody Beattie*

Resilient people learn from their experiences. They do not mentally beat themselves up and punish themselves for poor decisions or errors of judgement. They simply acknowledge the point, look for the learning in the experience, take it on board and then move on. They also recognise and celebrate their successes along the way, however small they may be. The importance of celebrating your successes shouldn't be underestimated. It helps you in the process of learning to nurture a positive view of yourself, which is an important part of your Bounce-back Ability. It also increases your awareness of the relationship between your actions and your successes. After all, it is very easy to fall into the trap of thinking and believing that you have not accomplished anything. People get so caught up in their lives that they forget how far they have come. It is vital to take a step back every now and again and reflect on your achievements. My little notebook that I write my three positives for the day helps with this, re-reading earlier entries helps me to get a sense of perspective and gives my self-confidence a lovely boost. I also take time at the end of each year to write down my accomplishments. Even little things, like finally clearing the garage, go on the list as well as big things, like passing exams and spending quality time with family.

Every little success helps to boost your confidence; if you have achieved this one thing, perhaps you can achieve something else. Recognising success, however small, helps you not to be discouraged by setbacks and reinforces your belief in yourself providing, motivation to keep going.

Plus, if you do not admit your successes to yourself, how can you expect others to be aware of them. A trap I have fallen into in the past is expecting other people to give me praise and feedback. How can they do this if they do not fully appreciate how difficult a task or situation was to me? It is up to me to recognise this, acknowledge my achievement and then share it so that others can celebrate with me.

Take a Moment for Personal Reflection Number 7

Grab a pen and paper and write yourself a list of everything you have achieved so far in your life, especially things you are proud of. From learning to ride a bike, to passing your driving test. The size of the achievement does not matter. The purpose of this, is to get you recognising your successes and for you to start to see where your strengths lie. If you want to take it a step further, then email your friends and family and ask them to list three things they believe are your strengths and what they think is your greatest success so far.

Learning Point

This is a lovely heart-warming exercise and can throw up some great surprises. In truth, it is our friends and family who can be a better judge of our character and talents then we can be. This is because our self-image can be distorted by the beliefs we hold about ourselves. These beliefs limit us, and our perception of past experiences colour our lives and our judgement.

Celebrate your successes & nurture an attitude of gratitude

I have mentioned in earlier chapters that keeping a journal, or a book of daily positives, is very beneficial. Obviously, this is a great way of tracking your achievements and recognising obstacles that you have overcome.

Another great tip is, when you achieve your small milestones, to give yourself a physical reward. I am not talking huge expensive gifts to you here; rather it's the simple pleasures that can give the most reward. For example, when I am doing paperwork, which is not a task I enjoy, I reward myself with an extra 30-minute lunch break or a cup of tea from my favourite teashop, if I get my paperwork done on time and with no procrastination. If I have had a particularly gruelling week, then I try to ensure that at the weekend I take time to do something for myself, for my enjoyment. This can be as simple as going to the cinema with a friend or taking my dog for an extra-long walk on the South Downs. Rewarding yourself and celebrating success is a natural follow-on from setting your goals and moving forward one step at a time. Also, it is easier to remember our accomplishments if we mark them along the way with celebrations, big or small. Like everything we have spoken about so far in this book, the important link is to believe you can do it, take the steps to do it, keep the momentum up and have patience. Rome wasn't built in a day and it takes time to build up your Bounce-back Ability.

Be sure to celebrate and be grateful for your life, as you ride that rollercoaster we call life.

An 'attitude of gratitude' is a wonderful attitude to cultivate to help build your Bounce-back Ability. Research by Dr Robert Emmons, a psychologist, showed that grateful people have higher levels of positive emotions, vitality, optimism and life satisfaction. They also have lower levels of depression and stress. All of which, points to having an attitude of gratitude as being an essential part of your Bounce-back Ability toolkit.

All of us have many things to be grateful for, even when the rollercoaster of life is throwing us around. Sadly, some people only realise this when they have lost something or someone important to them. Don't wait; take time now to appreciate the good in situations and people. It is rare that a situation or person is as black and white as, good or bad. It is us that label these things in this way, so let's stop labelling them and start being more grateful.

Stop, and think of as many things as you can that you are thankful for right now. List them on a piece of paper or a notebook. From the roof over your head to the clothes on your back, to the sun coming up each morning. We all have many wonderful things in our lives, big and small. Listing them shows you just how much you have. The more you start to train your brain to look for what is right, rather than what is wrong the more gratitude you will start to feel. Go on try it. Do it for 21 days and see if it doesn't make a difference.

Oprah Winfrey summed up the importance of gratitude when she said:

> *"It's not easy being grateful all the time. But it's when you feel least thankful that you are most in need of what gratitude can give you."*
> Oprah Winfrey

Top tips for celebrating success and developing an attitude of gratitude

1. **Share your success** with someone who can appreciate what went into your achievement however big or small. Celebrating with a friend is so much more rewarding than on your own. A reciprocal arrangement of mutual appreciation of success is a lovely bond to feed the growth of friendship.

2. **Smile**. When you smile, you release feel-good chemicals that increase your positive feelings. Which, in turn, increases your motivation,, increases your confidence, and increases your resilience. So find time each day to smile at your success and those moments of gratitude. If you don't feel much like smiling then stick a little coloured sticker in a number of places around your house, like by the kettle, on the bathroom mirror, on your car keys etc. Then whenever you see the stickers, make yourself smile. Remember your brain does not know real from unreal, so it will release those feel-good chemicals. I read about the smile stickers in a book by Paul McKenna and tried it; it worked brilliantly.

3. **Write a letter of appreciation**. If keeping a journal or a gratitude diary, which I have mentioned in previous tips, is not your thing, then try writing a letter. You can write it to whomever you want to thank; God, the Universe, a friend. Whom you write to is not as important as the act of doing it. The aim is to just get the thoughts of appreciation flowing. You don't have to post it if you don't want to. However, gratitude is contagious, you catch it from other people and they catch it from you. When you live with gratitude, it brings happiness, others see that and soon they are grateful. Before you know it, you have started an epidemic of gratitude. How amazing is that?

4. **To Do List**. The biggest mistake you can make is to think that an accomplishment is too small and dismiss it. The simple act of having even the small things listed on a To Do List, means you can tick things off as you go. This gives you feedback and an opportunity to give yourself credit and reward.

5. **Relaxation**. Simply taking ten minutes each day to relax and empty your mind can be a reward in itself. You can do this lying in a warm bath at the end of a busy day, pausing for ten minutes on a

park bench when walking the dog, or simply stopping for a cup of tea. It is not how you do it that is important; it is actually doing it.

6. **Volunteering**. We all lead busy lives, but being busy should not be an excuse not to help others. Helping others helps the helper and there is lots of research to back this fact up. When you volunteer, you find out more about yourself and your capabilities. Self-discovery is another resilience tool to help you build your Bounce-back Ability; we will look at it in more detail in a later chapter. Volunteering may well be challenging, but the challenge helps you to acquire skills that enable you to face the difficulties in your own life with more confidence and self-belief. So it's a win-win scenario. You can also learn new skills that may give you qualifications to help you find a new path in life. When you volunteer, you will most certainly meet new people who can help inspire you. This also strengthens the feeling of community and belonging, another excellent resilient tool.

To find out more about volunteering check out these websites:

http://timebank.org.uk or http://www.wrvs.org.uk

"To speak gratitude is courteous and pleasant, to enact gratitude is generous and noble, but to live gratitude is to touch heaven"

Johannes A Gaetner

Chapter Six

Be connected and supported

> *"Lots of people want to ride with you in the limo, but what you want is someone who will take the bus with you when the limo breaks down."*
> *Oprah Winfrey*

Being connected and supported by others has significant benefits to emotional and mental wellbeing and there is plenty of research to support this. In fact, Abraham Maslow, a psychologist, developed a hierarchy of human needs, which has love and belonging firmly in the centre.

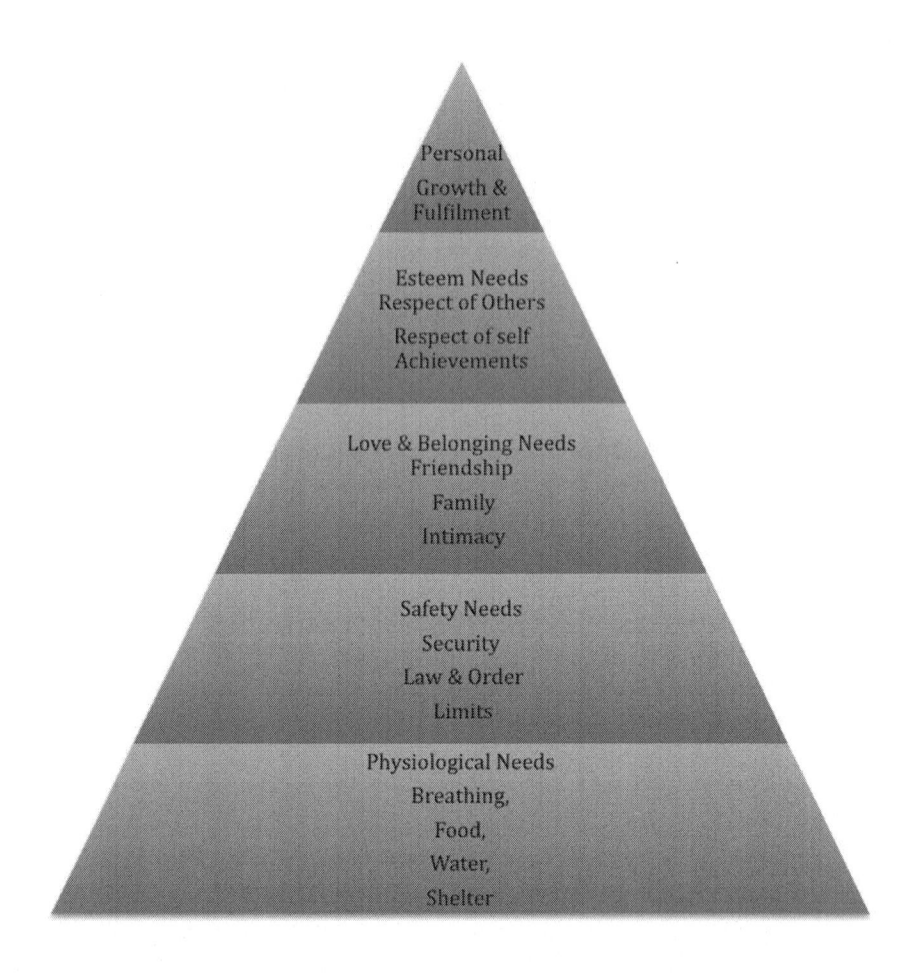

```
              Personal
              Growth &
              Fulfilment

           Esteem Needs
          Respect of Others
           Respect of self
           Achievements

        Love & Belonging Needs
             Friendship
               Family
              Intimacy

           Safety Needs
             Security
            Law & Order
              Limits

        Physiological Needs
            Breathing,
              Food,
              Water,
             Shelter
```

Diagram 8 - Maslow's Hierarchy of Needs

Love and belonging are one of our fundamental needs as a human being, along with food, water and shelter. Indeed having caring, supportive people around us, acts as a protective buffer to the impact of the ups and downs of life's rollercoaster. This is another key part of your Bounce-back Ability strategy. One of the reasons I lost my bounce was because I lost three very significant people in my life in a short space of time. First, my Dad to cancer, then my relationship broke down, and then my best friend lost her fight with cancer. Thankfully, my family and friends understood and were supportive. However, I also realised that I needed to build new friendships and connections as I had become quite isolated. A significant proportion of my social life had been entwined in my relationship and I had neglected other friendships in favour of being with my best friend and my family. I was also self-employed so did not have a work community either. It was not unsurprising that my resilience was shaken. Being aware of this has meant that I could put in place measures to develop more connections with my local community and with local organisations, as well as nurturing my existing relationships with friends and family.

Measures I took included agreeing to run the local AOR area support group for reflexologists; this has helped me to develop a stronger support community within my work. I also joined a local business-networking group and started ballet lessons. As a lone parent, it can be difficult juggling time for my social life along with the necessary mum duties and responsibilities that are part of parenthood. As a result, my social life is not currently as active as I would like, but I am aware of this and I am making plans, which is the main thing.

Having good relationships with your family and your friends is important. They know and understand you; they can help put things into perspective. Simply talking and sharing feelings with them does not make your troubles go away, but it helps get them off your chest and helps them to understand what you are going through. When they offer help and support, it can be tempting to say "no thank you,, I'm fine really". But it is important to consider the offer carefully, for accepting help from those that care about you will strengthen your resilience.

This temptation to batten down the hatches and to isolate yourself in the belief that you can cope, or that your friends have enough of their own troubles to deal with, without you adding yours on top is something I know I was guilty of. I don't know whether it was pride in not wanting to ask for help, or fear that if someone were kind to me I would wobble and unleash a torrent of tears. I now understand and acknowledge that my resilience was low because of the way I had isolated myself. Caring and supporting is part of the role of good family and friends, but by isolating ourselves, we deprive them of this role.

The need to feel valued and useful to others is an important part of our humanity; it gives back as much as it takes in terms of emotional wellbeing and energy. Choosing to isolate may give you a momentary sense of safety, especially if you are recovering from a broken relationship, but you will pay a heavy price for it in terms of your mental wellbeing. If you remain locked away in your own emotional tower for any length of time, you will weaken your resilience. Also the longer you disconnect from people, the harder it can be to reconnect. Being emotionally connected to people is like a muscle; if we don't use it, it will wither and become weak. Being emotionally connected is a vital part of being human.

Another way to become connected is to help others. Assisting others can help you to help yourself. It helps to put your own troubles into perspective; it will allow you to focus on something other than your own problems. This act in itself can free up your thinking to be more creative in terms of problem solving. For me, when I was looking at ways to help others I volunteered to help out with a charity that I am passionate about, Tamba, Twins and Multiple Birth Association http://www.tamba.org.uk. It was very fortunate that at the time I made this decision, Tamba were looking to recruit members as volunteers to facilitate seminars for parents who are expecting twins, triplets or more. For me it was a perfect fit; I am a mother of twin girls, I am passionate about empowering parents, and I love presenting and training. Running the seminars every three months has been a brilliant way for me to help my favourite charity, help expectant parents and help myself too. It's a win-win situation all round as they say.

Being amongst people who have been in similar situations can also be very supportive. They can have a greater depth of understanding about your situation than maybe friends or family can, because they too are experiencing similar emotions and experiences. This helps to create a sense of community and bonds people together allowing them to be mutually supportive. If a local support group does not exist then try starting your own, as you can be sure you are not as alone as you may feel you are.

Channelling anger and injustice into a more positive way is the starting point for many a new charity or good cause. It helps to focus the negative emotions into a more positive constructive format and inspires change for the better. Thankfully, in this age of computers and the internet we can connect with like-minded individuals all over the world. Whilst it is better to be connected face to face with real life people, so we can see their expressions and body language and feel their touch, this is not always easily possible. If there is someone a thousand or so miles away that we can connect with who understands what we are going through then that has to be a huge benefit of the internet.

Spending time with people who are upbeat, positive and interesting is also great. After all, mood can be infectious and it can really help to lift you if you are having a bad day. A cautionary word though, don't turn to friends in order to just have a good moan. Get it off your chest, by all means, but don't continue to bang on about it without actually making the necessary changes in your life to move you forward. People who moan and groan constantly are called energy vampires for a reason; they drain us of our emotional energy. So, whilst it is important to sound off, you also have to use your energy to help yourself find solutions. You can do it, we are all stronger than we realise. As Christopher Robin said to Winnie the Pooh:

> *"You're braver than you believe, stronger than you seem, and smarter than you think."*
> *Christopher Robin*

Take a Moment for Personal Reflection Number 8

Take five minutes to think about where your main support systems are and how connected and supported you feel.

Here are some questions to ask yourself:

1. Do you have friends who live close by?

2. Do you see them regularly?

3. Do you have friends who you speak to regularly, but see infrequently?

4. If so, when was the last time you met up?

5. Who is the person you pick up the phone to when you have a worry?

6. Is this the same person you ring when you have triumph or good news to share?

7. Do you feel supported and connected?

8. Do you have hobbies that you enjoy and that you do regularly?

9. If you could do one thing to make life more enjoyable, what would it be?

Learning Point

The purpose of this exercise is simply to raise your awareness and for you to see if you can improve your connections and support.

If you mainly answered no to the questions, then you should consider putting in place some of the tips from the next section.

Another question you can ask yourself to further develop your connections and supports is:

If you could do one thing to make your support systems better, what would it be?

Top tips on how to build your connections and support systems

1. **Become 'a joiner'** - Join local clubs, conservation groups, any association that you are interested in or passionate about etc. Shared passions and interests help to bond people. Buy your local newspaper to find out what's on in your local community or check out local online sites to find out what's on in your area like http://www.localpeople.co.uk

2. **Get out and about** – Reacquaint yourself with your local area by leaving the car at home and going for a walk. As you walk look up, head held high striding out at a comfortable pace, try not to look down. Depressed people walk slowly looking down, avoiding eye contact with people. So by looking up you change your physiology to a more positive one and this will simply help you feel more positive. Plus you will see, hear, and feel, things you may previously have missed. Smile, and say hello as you pass people, smiling helps you feel good. I have found that, since getting a dog, I now know lots more people in my

community and I love my daily walks as much as my dog does.

3. **Volunteer** - Do you have causes or charities that resonate with you, that you feel connected to? Voluntary organisations and charities need your support. They rely heavily on volunteers and are flexible about how much time you need to give. It is amazing how mutually beneficial the relationship can be to both parties. Go on, give it a try; you have nothing to lose.

4. **Friendships, be proactive** - When people are busy they get in the habit of only contacting friends when they need something. Give friends a call just to see how they are doing. Alternatively send them an email, post them a funny postcard you spotted and make them smile, write on their wall on Facebook or just pick up the phone. Even if you have been isolating yourself, it is never too late to reconnect.

"In everyone's life, at some time, our inner fire goes out. It is then burst into flames by an encounter with another human being. We should all be grateful to those people who rekindle the inner spirit"

Albert Schweitzer

Chapter Seven

Nurture your mind, body and spirit

> "Breathe. Let go. And remind yourself that this very moment is the only one you know you have for sure."
> Oprah Winfrey

Finally and most importantly, the last piece of the Bounce-back Ability Tool Kit is learning to nurture yourself. By this, I mean that you look after your whole self, your mind, your body and your spirit.

All too often, our lives are very busy and we run around looking after everyone else, friends, family, work colleagues and we put ourselves at the bottom of the priority list. When challenged on this, many people say that they are just too busy, that they do not have any spare cash to spend on treats for themselves, they do not have time, the kids, husband, wife, work must come first, etc. The truth of the matter is that you can't afford *not* to take time for nurturing yourself. For, if you neglect yourself, at best you are not meeting your full potential and at worst you run the risk of exhaustion, burnout and illness. No one is immune from the cumulative effects of long-term stress that comes with running on full throttle.

Brain scans of busy people have shown that the emotional areas of their brains are constantly on high alert. This is a huge drain on the energy and resources available to the brain. No wonder people experience headaches, tiredness and mood swings.

Stress is a much-used word, and according to a survey in 2011 from the Chartered Institute of Personal Development, it is now the number one cause of workplace absence. Stress is our body's natural response to a threat; it is a primitive response designed to protect us from sabre-toothed tigers. It is commonly referred to as the flight or fight response. In modern life, we seldom come across life-threatening situations, like being chased by sabre-toothed tigers. A modern life-threatening situation is more likely to be slamming your brakes on to avoid a collision with another car, or running away from a mugger. Most modern stress is in fact down to our perception of a situation. For example, we get stressed about meeting work deadlines, giving a speech or worrying about finances and job stability.

Not all stress is bad though; in fact, stress can also be empowering and positive and is called eustress. An example of eustress is the adrenaline surge that an actor gets before going on stage to give a live performance, or an athlete gets before a big race. It helps us to push the limits and give our all to a situation.

The fight or flight response kicks in whether the stress is good or bad. As soon as we perceive something to be stressful, the response kicks in. Signals from the brain cause the release of chemical messengers (hormones) adrenaline and cortisol. These messengers trigger off dramatic changes in the body as it prepares to either run or fight.

The following diagram shows the changes that happen.

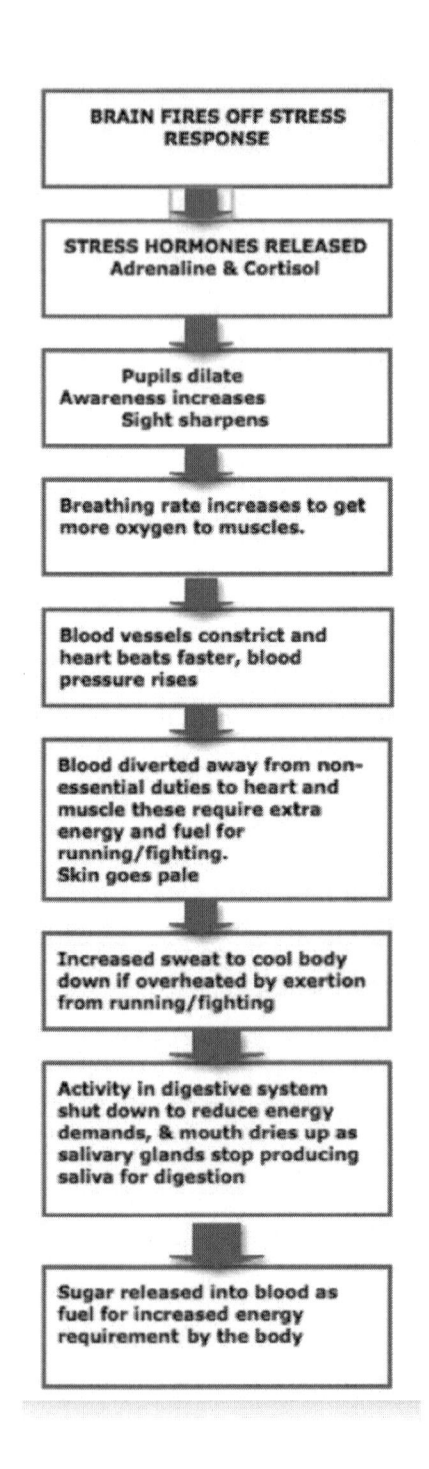

```
┌─────────────────────────────┐
│   BRAIN FIRES OFF STRESS    │
│          RESPONSE           │
└─────────────────────────────┘
              ▼
┌─────────────────────────────┐
│  STRESS HORMONES RELEASED   │
│     Adrenaline & Cortisol   │
└─────────────────────────────┘
              ▼
┌─────────────────────────────┐
│       Pupils dilate         │
│    Awareness increases      │
│       Sight sharpens        │
└─────────────────────────────┘
              ▼
┌─────────────────────────────┐
│ Breathing rate increases to │
│ get more oxygen to muscles. │
└─────────────────────────────┘
              ▼
┌─────────────────────────────┐
│ Blood vessels constrict and │
│ heart beats faster, blood   │
│ pressure rises              │
└─────────────────────────────┘
              ▼
┌─────────────────────────────┐
│ Blood diverted away from    │
│ non-essential duties to     │
│ heart and muscle these      │
│ require extra energy and    │
│ fuel for running/fighting.  │
│ Skin goes pale              │
└─────────────────────────────┘
              ▼
┌─────────────────────────────┐
│ Increased sweat to cool     │
│ body down if overheated by  │
│ exertion from running/      │
│ fighting                    │
└─────────────────────────────┘
              ▼
┌─────────────────────────────┐
│ Activity in digestive       │
│ system shut down to reduce  │
│ energy demands, & mouth     │
│ dries up as salivary glands │
│ stop producing saliva for   │
│ digestion                   │
└─────────────────────────────┘
              ▼
┌─────────────────────────────┐
│ Sugar released into blood   │
│ as fuel for increased       │
│ energy requirement by the   │
│ body                        │
└─────────────────────────────┘
```

Diagram 9 - The changes in the body during flight or fight response

The heart rate and breathing rate increase as the body diverts resources to the muscles and limbs so that they are primed and ready for action. The pupils dilate, sight sharpens, awareness increases, impulses quicken, and the perception of pain diminishes as the body prepares for action. We scan and search our environment looking for the enemy. Because our fight or flight system is activated, we tend to perceive everything in our environment as a possible threat to our survival. By its very nature the fight or flight system bypasses our rational mind, (our rational mind is the logical reasoning mind) and this moves us into attack mode. Even our IQ drops by up to 20 points. When you understand this, you realise why normally mild mannered people can end up thumping a complete stranger in a road rage incident.

When we face real dangers to our physical survival, the fight or flight response is invaluable. In modern life, it is only events that we perceive to be threats that trigger the flight or fight activation, e.g. being asked to meet a tight work deadline. On a daily basis, stress hormones flow into our bodies to deal with events that pose no real threat to our physical survival. In the long term, this can be very harmful to our health.

In most of today's situations, once our fight or flight response is activated, we cannot fight or flee. We sit in our office or home and 'deal with it'. In short, the situations we perceive as threats, trigger a response that causes us to become aggressive, hyper-vigilant and over-reactive. It is counterproductive for us to punch our boss (the fight response), or run away (flight response), when we perceive a request for tighter deadlines from the boss to be a threat. This leads to a situation where we build up stress hormones in the body. If these are not broken down it can lead to disorders of the nervous system, immune system and hormone imbalances (headaches, irritable bowels, high blood pressure, chronic fatigue, allergies, increased premenstrual syndrome symptoms to name but a few).

This long-term stress and its effects on the body have been researched and categorised into three stages by Audrey Livingstone Booth.

These stages are shown in the following diagram.

STAGE 1 — ALARM
- The activation of flight or fight response
- When threat is removed body returns to normal state
- If threat not removed or stress hormones not burnt off stage 2 commences

STAGE 2 — RESISTANCE
- When the perception of the threat continues for a long period of time the body will strive for balance
- The body releases more stress hormones into the blood
- The body may not fully utilise these hormones and physical, emotional and mental capabilities decline
- Feelings of tiredness and anxiety occur and quick fixes like alcohol, drugs and destructive behaviour occur
- If dealt with individual can return to normal state with no long term effects
- If not stage 3 commences

STAGE 3 — EXHAUSTION
- The body is unable to use the stress chemicals effectively. The body is using energy faster than it can be replaced. When energy supplies run out the individual suffers exhaustion
- The immune system becomes affected making the body open to infection. Research has also linked cancer to long term stress. In addition stress related conditions such as depression may be experienced. Once dealt with the individual may recover. However long term effects can remain

Diagram 10 - The three stages of stress

*Nurture your mind, body and spirit - **133***

Take a Moment for Personal Reflection Number 9

Take a moment to reflect on what you have learnt about stress.

1. **Do you recognise which stage you are at? Be honest with yourself.**

2. **Are you aware of what triggers you to get stressed? Is it your boss? Is it your daily commute? Is it the kids arguing over the games console?**

3. **Do you need to make changes in the way you perceive stress?**

4. Do you need to make changes in the way you handle stress?

Learning point

This moment of reflection will have raised your awareness of your stress triggers and how you handle stress. To simplify this, here's my ABC approach (Awareness, Belief, and Commitment to change) to managing stress:

Step 1: Awareness of what and where, your stress triggers are, is the first step to managing your stress.

Step 2: Belief that you can manage your stress.

Step 3: Commitment that you will change your responses, manage your emotions, and handle your stress better.

If you need help with making those changes, consult a professional medical practitioner or therapist.

I used to be a classic example of someone who put everyone else first and neglected myself. Even when my body was screaming at me that I needed to pace myself better, I ignored it. This neglect resulted in recurrent coughs and colds, cold sores, the symptoms from my polycystic ovary syndrome (PCOS) got significantly worse, and I looked and felt constantly tired. I knew I had to make adjustments and the exacerbation of my PCOS symptoms was the push I needed to do that.

But where to start was the big question. I was a lone parent with three young primary school age kids. I was working full time as a company director and my schedule was booked out from 5.30am to gone 10pm at night, most days. Worse still, I was putting everyone else's needs before mine. Even I had to acknowledge that things had to change, for if my health worsened the situation would develop into a crisis.

I have always been interested in complimentary therapies, and decided to try reflexology as a way to help relax and to rebalance my stressed out body. Fortunately, I found a local reflexologist who did home visits. I started to have regular treatments on a Saturday morning. The kids would watch a DVD and my reflexologist would come round and give me a one-hour treatment in the comfort of my own home.

Reflexology is a complimentary health therapy that uses a specific technique on the feet to help the body to restore its natural balance. It is a very relaxing therapy and that one-hour was the only hour of the week that was really mine.

Having regular treatments (initially weekly, then every two weeks, then monthly maintenance treatments) not only improved my wellbeing, my PCOS symptoms reduced and I stopped getting recurrent coughs and colds. Taking time 'for me' also acted as a catalyst that then enabled me to put in place small changes to my diet, lifestyle, and attitude to myself, that helped me to get a better balanced life.

In fact, I loved reflexology so much, that after the business I was a director of was sold, I decided to have a career change. I went and trained as a reflexologist and started my own practice.

If you are interested in reflexology you can check out the Association of Reflexologists website for information and local qualified therapists http://www.aor.org.uk/home/what-is-reflexology.

Other complimentary therapies are available and can help with relaxation and managing stress. Ensure your practitioner is qualified, insured and check with your doctor that that any medical conditions you have are not contraindicated.

Check out http://www.nhstadirectory.org or http://www.the-cma.org.uk/

The important lesson that this experience taught me, is that it is possible to make the necessary changes to get life more balanced. You just have to know that you need to make changes, decide you are going to make those changes, believe you can do it, and then take it one step at a time. Factoring in time for nurturing and self-care is not only possible it is essential.

The simplest way to get started is to start paying attention to yourself and your own needs. This can be difficult for some people, Psychologists' call this being outer-directed. The primary concern of outer-directed people is for the needs of others and their relationship with the people they care for. Nurturing others and building relationships is their guiding principle. Not unsurprisingly, many women are outer-directed.

Inner-directed people, have their own internal guidance system that helps them focus on what is best for them, before everything else. Their self-interest is high and they frequently put their own needs above others.

Ideally, we need to have a balance of both inner and outer direction in our lives. This is possible to achieve by raising our awareness, acknowledging the need to change, and then taking steps to be more inner-directed. Sometimes putting yourself and your needs first may feel strange at the start, but it is crucial that we all learn to self-nurture. Friends and family that genuinely care for you can help you, as you learn this vital part of resilience. I am not suggesting that you suddenly become selfish and self-focused, but that you simply find some balance by taking time for personal nurturing.

As you have been reading this chapter you may have started to form some realisations about yourself and may have recognised whether you are inner or outer directed. Getting to know and understand 'you' is another part of the nurturing process. How well do you know yourself? Have you ever stopped and taken the opportunity to get to know and understand yourself?

Start the process of getting to know you better, by completing the next 'Take a moment for personal reflection'. Remember there are no right or wrong answers.

Take a Moment for Personal Reflection Number 10

Getting to know yourself better, starts with asking yourself the following questions. This will help you to find and celebrate your strengths, reflect upon areas of your life that you want to change and start to formulate ways to improve your self-nurture.

Work through the following questions one by one. Leave any that you find difficult to answer, and come back to them later. Be aware that, if it is difficult to answer, then that particular question is probably challenging you in some way, so it is even more important to answer it at some point. Discussing it with a trusted friend, loved one, or a therapist, can help you discover more about yourself. Remember there are no right or wrong answers to these questions.

1. **Who is the most important person / people in your life and why?**

2. **Are you spending the quality time with them that you want to?**

3. If not, what one action could you take today to change that?

4. Will you take that action today? If not when will you? Put a date down and stick to it.

5. Write down, in the space below, your greatest achievement so far in your life?

6. What else would you like to achieve in your lifetime?

7. Have you ever asked your friends and family what they like best about you? If not go ahead and do it, it can be an eye-opener.

8. What do you think are your best qualities?

9. How do you spend your leisure time?

10. What are your favourite activities / pastimes?

11. Do you get time to partake in those activities on a regular basis?

12. If not, what one action could you take today to change that?

13. On a scale of 1 to 10, how much do you enjoy your work? (1 is 'not at all', 10 is 'love it')

14. If you could have any job, what would it be?

15. Are you putting off doing certain things? Are you putting any areas / difficulties of your life on hold? If so, why?

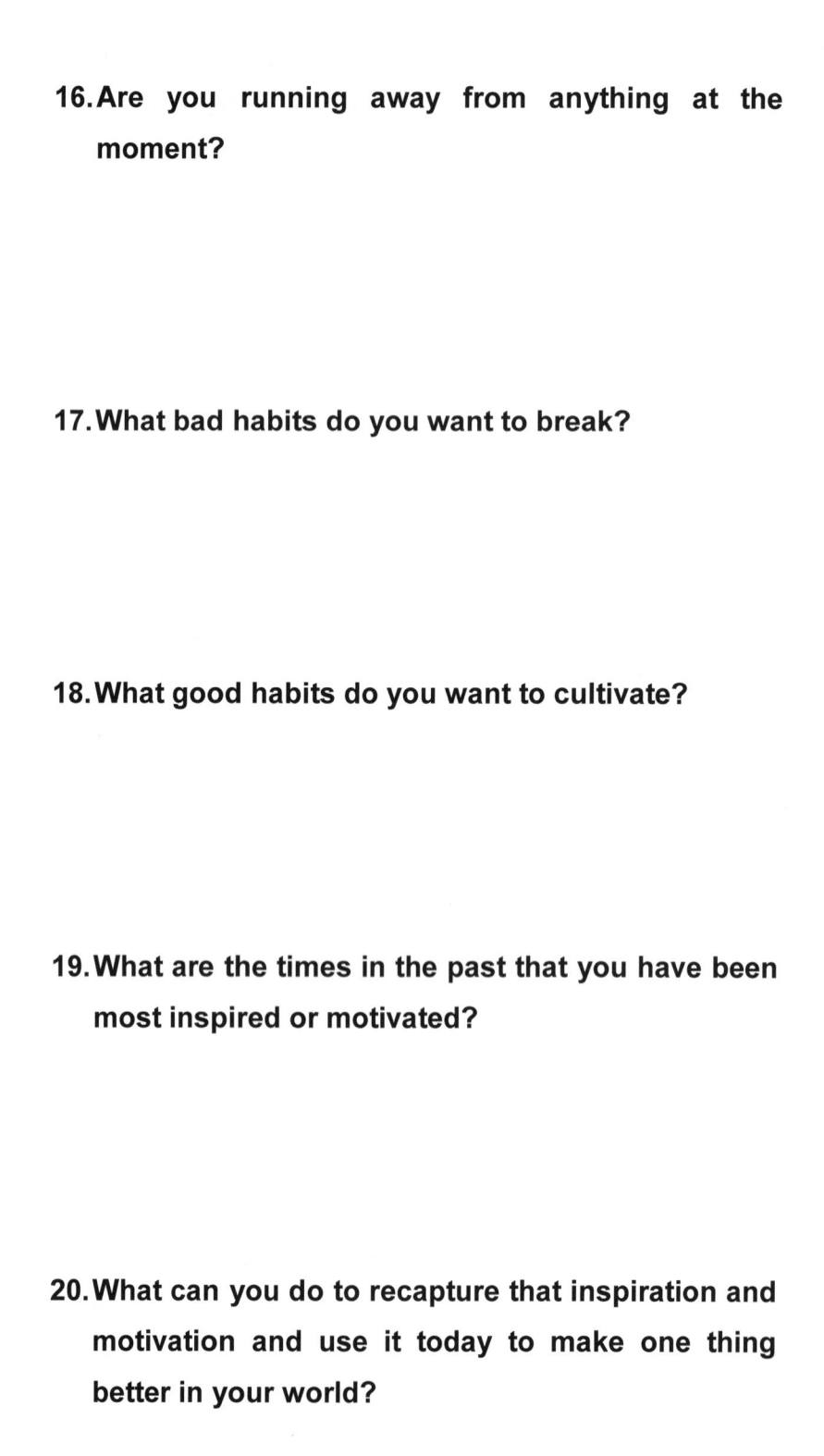

16. Are you running away from anything at the moment?

17. What bad habits do you want to break?

18. What good habits do you want to cultivate?

19. What are the times in the past that you have been most inspired or motivated?

20. What can you do to recapture that inspiration and motivation and use it today to make one thing better in your world?

21. Who are the people you spend most time with?

22. Are these people positive influences on your life, will they support you in your efforts to nurture yourself?

23. Do you eat a healthy balanced diet?

24. If not, what one action could you take today to improve your eating habits?

25. Do you drink alcohol to help you unwind?

Nurture your mind, body and spirit - **145**

26. If yes, can you think of another way to unwind that will be healthier?

27. Are you willing to take action and make changes so that you can nurture yourself more?

> **Learning point**
>
> Understanding yourself better will help you identify the changes needed in your life. So that you can work towards living a more balanced life and building your Bounce-back Ability.

As human beings, we are far more than just a collection of working parts. Our mind, body, and spirit, are all interconnected and none work in isolation. In this book, we have looked at the brain chemistry of negative and positive thinking. And how those thoughts trigger the release of hormones. We also know that, how we stand and move, will affect our moods and that, if we perceive that a situation is a threat to us, we trigger our stress response.

This area of research into 'the mind body connection' continues to grow as technology allows us to delve further into the connections of the brain. Research shows that the brain is divided into two hemispheres, each with different specialist functions and responsible for controlling different sides of the body. In simple terms, the right side of the brain specialises in pictures, emotions, and creativity, and it controls the left side of the body. The left side of the brain specialises in logic, language, and it analyses and controls the right side of the body.

The brain also operates various brainwave frequencies and research has linked these to states of consciousness.

- **Beta** - the band we operate in when awake and conscious.

- **Alpha** - the frequency we run when asleep. It is involved in creative process, problem solving, dreams, and healing. This is the level reached during meditation

- **Theta** - this frequency is accessed during deep meditation and also during sleep.

- **Delta** - the slowest frequency accessed during very deep sleep and unconsciousness.

We run alpha, theta and delta during a good night's sleep and it is the power of those on our body that makes a good night's sleep so restorative. Likewise, if we are not getting enough good quality sleep, a) because we are going to bed too late or getting up too early, or b) because we are awake fretting and worrying, then it is easy to see why poor sleep is detrimental to our mental and physical wellbeing. Good quality sleep is another part of nurturing yourself. I have included some tips on sleep in the top tip section at the end of the chapter.

Other ways to nurture the mind are, to learn to relax deeply, and to learn to meditate.

It sounds so simple, but like so many things in modern life we do have to take the time to learn these skills and then practice the technique. The great thing about the relaxation response is that it counteracts the stress response, thereby lowering the level of stress hormones and lowering the heart rate and blood pressure. It is a technique that is extremely beneficial and one that you can learn to bring about yourself.

Both relaxation and meditation start with learning good breathing. It is amazingly simple, but incredibly powerful and hugely beneficial to your health. When you are tense, you breathe without engaging your full lung capacity. This means the lowest part of your lungs does not get its full share of oxygenated air, which increases heart rate and increases anxiety. When you breathe deeply you engage all the breathing muscles, expand the lungs fully and fill the lungs with oxygenated air. This lowers heart rate and blood pressure.

A simple breathing exercise is to put your hands on your belly and take a deep breath in through your nose. As you breathe in, feel your hands moving apart as your abdomen expands and your lungs fill with air. Breathe in, to the count of three and out to the count of four. Repeat three times. Do this simple exercise whenever tension is rising and it will soon become second nature. To get even better results try extending the out breath to five then six.

Meditation is the ability to train the mind to induce a state of consciousness that is free from scattered thoughts. Historically, it has been associated closely with some religions and with activities like yoga. However, psychology research on its benefits for mental and emotional wellbeing, have recently bought it more into the mainstream arena. Typically, when a person meditates they are in a quiet space, sitting comfortably and breathing slowly and deeply as they free the mind of thoughts. If you have ever been so deeply engrossed in an activity that you have lost complete track of time and awareness of external activities then you have been doing a type of meditation known as activity meditation without even knowing it. Well done, you can meditate and you didn't even know it. Learning to meditate is a lovely way to nurture your mind, body and spirit and it is very accessible with both local groups and free online access.

Check out the Mental Health Foundation UK site, at:

> http://www.bemindful.co.uk/about_mindfulness

Or, my favourite, which combines meditation and mindfulness:

> http://www.getsomeheadspace.com/

Mindfulness is a way of paying attention to the moment of now. You bring your attention to the present moment in a non-judgmental accepting way. This helps you to become more connected to your thoughts and feelings related to whatever you are doing.

> *"Mindfulness meditation has demonstrated beneficial effects on the brain and the immune system."*
> *Prof R Davidson*
> *Professor of psychiatry university of Wisconsin*

I recommend that you look at ways that you can integrate relaxation, mindfulness and meditation into your life. I can assure you that your mind, body and spirit will benefit.

The best advice I was ever given that helped me understand how to nurture myself, was that I needed to learn to act as if I was my own best friend.

Top tips for nurturing mind, body and spirit

1. **Eat a healthy diet, and exercise.** There are plenty of dietary advice books out there and it can be extremely confusing as to what exactly one should be doing. I like to apply a KISS approach (Keep it simple, stupid). So firstly, make sure you keep your body hydrated. Your body needs two litres of fluid a day to carry out its daily work of breathing, digesting and excreting. That fluid should, where possible, be caffeine and alcohol free. Simply because too much of either have a negative impact on your body. The very best drink to have is, of course, water. I always start and finish my day with a glass of water and try to have water with meals. The next piece of simple advice is to make sure your plate has plenty of colourful vegetables on it. The more colour reds, dark greens, purples the more packed full of healthy nutrients they are. Contrary to popular belief, we do not need to have meat everyday as long as we get plenty of protein, via nuts, pulses and vegetables. We were not designed to eat meat every day. Back in our caveman days, we would have had plenty of meat-free days between

successful hunting parties. And carbohydrates, like pasta, rice and potatoes are great, but they should never fill more than 1/3 of your plate. For more detailed information checkout the NHS website http://www.nhs.uk/LiveWell/healthy-eating/Pages/Healthyeating.aspx

2. **Learn to say, "No!"** Are you the 'go to' person, the one that everyone always asks to help? Do you say "yes", because you don't want to upset people? Do you find you can end up letting people down, because you cannot meet all your commitments? If this is you, then you need to learn to say "No!". We all have limits to our time and energy, and whilst it's good to help others, it's also important that we keep our lives balanced. So how do we say no, without hurting people's feelings? In my experience politeness and courtesy is essential. So for example if you are asked to help out at yet another school event then try saying, "Thank you for considering me, it's an honour to be asked. However, I am very sorry I cannot commit to that this year." As ever, it takes practice and may raise a few eyebrows but you only have so much energy, so you and your family must come first.

3. **Learn something new.** Enriching your life with new knowledge is a great way to nurture yourself. It could be a new hobby or further education and both will benefit you. Check out your local schools and collages for course lists. I did a computing for the terrified course back in 1997 and it helped me to apply for a job as a nurse in an insurance company. That enabled me to get off benefits so it completely changed my life for the better.

4. **Learn to live in the moment.** Live life to the fullest by focusing your attention on what is happening now. Don't waste time and energy constantly looking forward to the next day off, next holiday, next whatever. Take a breath and look for the simple pleasures in today as well. It is good to have goals. We have talked about them and they are essential, but it is also important to enjoy the journey along the way and appreciate the moment of now. Spending too much energy focussing on the future can stop you enjoying the moment of now.

5. **Go on a journey of self-discovery.** Find out more about yourself and what is important to you. The better you know yourself the more you can help others, the more powerful you are in mind,

body and spirit. We have touched on it a few times in the book. Attending workshops, reading books or articles on topics of personal development that interest you will teach you lots about yourself.

6. **Laugh lots.** Laughter releases us from tension and anger. It pours endorphins, our feel good hormones into the blood stream. Laughter has even been found to speed up healing. A study of patients undergoing chemotherapy found that the group who listened or watched 1 hour of comedy a day had less side effects from the medication and made a quicker recovery. How amazing is that? I love the power of laughter. When I used to commute 50 miles each way to work I always kept a selection of comedy CD's in the car to listen to on the way home. In my opinion there is no better antidote to the stress of rush hour traffic.

7. **Don't try to control the uncontrollable.** Many things in life are beyond our direct control, especially the behaviours of others. Rather than letting them 'wind us up' choose to focus on what you can control, your reaction to that person or situation. Start by counting to ten, and then take a deep breath, before reframing the thought you are thinking into a more positive empowering one.

Then imagine creating a barrier between you and them that will protect you from their negativity. As soon as possible physically move yourself away from them.

8. **Do a little something for yourself each day.** Take time each day to do something for yourself that you enjoy. The simple pleasures are the best. Whether it is a nice 10-minute soak in the bath in peace and quiet, a walk in the park at lunchtime or a cup of tea drunk whilst still hot it does not matter. It is simply taking the time to be mindful of your needs and to indulge in simple pleasures that have been found to be most beneficial to good resilience. The important thing here is to believe that you are 'worth it'. Trust me you most certainly are.

9. **Get good night's sleep**.

    a. Start by having a regular routine. Go to bed at the same time each night and get up at the same time each day, even on weekends. If you have a late night a nap the next day is much better for you than a lie in. Having a lie in disrupts your sleep-wake rhythm.

b. Next make sure you spend time outside each day. Melatonin is the hormone that regulates the sleep-wake cycle. Its production is controlled by exposure to natural light. Make sure you get outside each day, try having a walk in your lunch break or taking your packed lunch to the park in the summer.

c. Setting up a relaxing bedtime routine helps your body to know its bedtime. Have a warm bath, do a few light stretching exercises, fill in your 3 positives in your diary, play some relaxing music and ensure your room is at optimum temperature for sleep (18-20 degree centigrade). Do not watch TV or use computers or smart phones before bed, they over stimulate and disrupt your sleep.

d. Avoid heavy meals late in the evening. Eating heavy meals late at night means the body is using lots of energy to digest food and this disrupts your sleep cycle. Reduce caffeine from midday. The effects of caffeine can last between 10-12 hours. Alcohol may help you fall asleep quickly but reduces the quality of your sleep so avoid alcohol. Some foods help induce sleep. These foods contain a protein called tryptophan which is a protein used to make serotonin (a feel good chemical that helps you relax). Have a bedtime snack of food containing tryptophan (turkey, milk, nuts and seeds) and combined with carbohydrate. This ensures the tryptophan gets to the brain quickly. The snack should be no more than 200 calories.

e. Finally lie down in your bed, take 2 or 3 deep breaths and visualise yourself relaxing, feeling calm, feeling sleepy and see yourself getting a good night's sleep. Remember, think about what you want, not what you don't.

And finally...

Remember that resilience matters

So there you have it, my take on resilience and my journey to get my bounce back. I consider myself to be a work in progress; there are always new insights to be gained, new skills to be learnt and new experiences to enjoy. My Bounce-back Ability continues to get stronger every day and my commitment to myself is to continue to learn about myself and develop it further.

I hope you have enjoyed what you learned from this book and have gained valuable insights into yourself. Remember each of us have extraordinary strengths, possibilities, courage, and stamina.

You may not always see it, but you really are stronger than you realise.

By continuing to develop your Bounce-back Ability you will continue to improve the quality of your life. And that will protect and buffer you from those sharp dips and turns on the rollercoaster of life.

One last moment for personal reflection, is for you to look back through the 'Moments For Reflection', earlier in the book. Be sure you know where your resilient strengths are, be aware of where the weaknesses lie, and then make a plan to take one step each day to strengthen your Bounce-back Ability. You can write them down in the next section, if you like.

Go boldly forward into your future, with a plan in your head, a spring in your step and a smile on your face.

Trust me, you really are worth it.

Personal Bounce-back Ability Plan

"Believe you can and you are halfway there."

Theodore Roosevelt

Personal Bounce-back Ability Plan

I commit to working on the following actions during the next month:

1.

2.

3.

Notes:

Signed:

Dated:

B.O.U.N.C.E.
The Bounce-back Ability Tool Kit

The Bounce-back Ability Tool Kit

The *'Bounce-back Ability Tool Kit'* comprises the following six **B.O.U.N.C.E.** components, each contained within the chapters of this book:

Belief in your ability to cope (See Chapter 1)

Optimism & goals (See Chapters 3 and 4)

s**U**rvival (See Chapter 2)

Nurture (See Chapter 7)

Connection & support (See Chapter 6)

Enjoyment of celebration and gratitude (See Chapter 5)

So make sure you work on all the different areas of B.O.U.N.C.E. and you will keep your Bounce-back Ability in tip-top shape.

For further information on formal B.O.U.N.C.E. workshops and training, please contact Helen via **www.cultive8.com**

Remember, once you have B.O.U.N.C.E., you have your Bounce-back Ability.

Important Notice

A number of times in this book, I stated that seeking professional support to help you manage balancing your stress, life and emotions is a good idea. And I really believe it is. Sadly, though some people do not find it easy to seek help. I would like us all to take responsibility for our minds health and well-being. Just like our bodies need to get help from the doctors when we feel unwell, sometimes our mind deserves help too.

I urge you to seek help if you are struggling by yourself. Sometimes, all it takes is the helping hand of a knowledgeable, caring professional to help, motivate, and support, you to get back on the path towards building your resilience.

If however you are experiencing any of the following please seek immediate help.

- Thoughts of death or suicide.

- Negative, or self-destructive, thoughts you cannot control.

- Using alcohol, food, or drugs, to help control difficult emotions.

- Feeling helpless, despair, and hopeless, most of the time.

- Chronic difficulty sleeping.

- Lack of ability to concentrate, to the point where it is affecting your work or home life.

Useful points of contact for help, guidance and support

The Samaritans:
http://www.samaritans.org
UK   08457 909090
ROI   1850 609090

Mind - The leading mental health charity for England & Wales

http://www.mind.org.uk/
0300 1233393

NHS Direct
http://www.nhsdirect.nhs.uk/
0845 4647

Bibliography

Bolte Taylor, Jill. *My stroke of Insight*. Great Britain: Hodder & Stoughton, 2008.

Emmons, R.A., & McCullough, M.E. *The psychology of gratitude*. USA: Oxford University Press, 2004.

Heppell, Michael. *Flipit*. Great Britain: Pearson Education Ltd, 2009.

Hitzges, Vicki. *Attitude Is Everything*. USA: Simple Truths, 2010

Kubler Ross, Elizabeth. *On Death & Dying*. Simon & Schuster/Touchstone, 1969.

Ledoux, Joseph. *The Emotional Brain: The mysterious underpinning of emotional life.* London: Orion Books Ltd, 1999.

Livingstone Booth, A. *Stressmanship*. London: Severn House, 1985.

Mayne, Brian. *Goal Mapping*. Great Britain: Watkins Publishing, 2006.

McKenna, Paul. *I Can Make You Happy*. Great Britain: Transworld Publishers, 2011.

Tracey, Brian. *Eat That Frog*. USA: Berrett.Koehlerr Publishers inc, 2001.

Richard. J. Davidson, Director and Antoine Lutz Associate Scientist. *Buddha's Brain: Neuroplasticity and Meditation.* IEEE Signal Process Mag. 2008 January 1; 25(1): 176–174.

François Lespérance, Nancy Frasure-Smith, Elise St-André, Gustavo Turecki, Paul Lespérance, Stephen R. Wisniewski. *The Efficacy of Omega-3 Supplementation for Major Depression: A Randomized Controlled Trial.* Journal of Clinical Psychiatry, 2010; DOI: 10.4088/JCP.10m05966blu.

McMillan, D.W., & Chavis, D.M. (1986). *Sense of community: A definition and theory.* Journal of Community Psychology, 14(1), 6-23.

Werner, E.E and Smith, R.S *Journeys from childhood to midlife: Risk, Resilience and Recovery.* USA, New York: Cornell University Press, 2001.

Web Sources:

CIPD survey, Nov 2011:
http://www.cipd.co.uk/research/_absence-management

http://dictionary.reference.com/browse/resilience

http://www.brainyquote.com/

Useful Websites

Information on volunteering

http://www.direct.gov.uk/en/HomeAndCommunity/Gettinginvolvedinyourcommunity/Volunteering/DG_064299

http://timebank.org.uk/

http://www.wrvs.org.uk

Local activities

http://www.localpeople.co.uk

Omega 3 supplements

http://www.mind1st.com/default.asp

Reflexology

http://www.aor.org.uk/home/what-is-reflexology.

Complimentary Therapies

http://www.nhstadirectory.org

http://www.the-cma.org.uk

Twins & Multiple Birth Association

http://www.tamba.org.uk

British Association for Counselling and Psychotherapy

http://www.bacp.co.uk

Healthy Eating

http://www.nhs.uk/LiveWell/healthy-eating/Pages/Healthyeating.aspx

Meditation

http://www.bemindful.co.uk/about_mindfulness

http://www.getsomeheadspace.com

About The Author

Helen Turier qualified as a Registered General Nurse in the Queen Alexandra's Royal Army Nursing Corp in 1989. After leaving the army, Helen focused her skills on her passion for education and training. Her personal rollercoaster has seen her go from being a lone parent with three pre-school children, living on social welfare, to becoming a director on the board of two successful companies within just five years.

After the sale of those companies, Helen took time to reconnect with her purpose. Her mission is to help people develop life balance and success, through reflexology, resilience and personal leadership.

Helen has been a professional trainer and speaker for over twelve years. And has helped individuals and businesses to develop the strategies and skills for a successful and resilient mindset for the last two years.

She knows and understands the skills and mindset required to juggle life's competing demands. And her insightful and inspirational style helps clients to take control, so they can achieve a successful and balanced life.

Helen is also a qualified Reflexologist and has been successfully practicing for the last five years.

> "Helen made me feel comfortable and explained carefully what she was doing. She answered my questions thoroughly and dealt with my reactions professionally. I enjoyed my treatments and felt the benefit of them on my health."
>
> **Mrs K. Jennings**

If you think that Helen could help you with one-to-one Resilience coaching or reflexology, then please contact her at helenturier@aol.com

For information on formal workshops and training for businesses, please contact Helen via www.cultive8.com

"I believe that each of us has extraordinary strengths, courage and stamina, although we may not always see it for ourselves. We really are stronger than we realise. My mission is to help people improve the quality of their life, simply by developing their capacity to cope with handling life's many twists and turns. You see, it's our 'Bounce-back Ability', or our ability to bounce back from adversity that protects and buffers us from the sharp dips and turns on the rollercoaster of life - making the ride much smoother and more fun. This book was written to help people learn from my personal experience, in the hope that they will gain some valuable insights to develop their own personal resilience."

Helen Turier RGN MAR

Cultive8

cultive8
GROWING POTENTIAL

Cultive8 delivers outstanding, thought provoking, and motivational, courses that build resilience, boost personal leadership, and encourage a 'can do' attitude across all areas of life.

Our courses focus on mind-set, not skill-set, clarifying vision and purpose at every level from board level to new recruits.

As business owners, Helen and the cultive8 team believe that it is essential to recognize that people are our number one asset. We believe business owners and managers have a duty of care to invest in their staff and support them in developing the right mind-set for today's fast changing world.

At Cultive8, it is our policy to give back to our local community and in particular to our young people - the entrepreneurs, leaders and employees of tomorrow. For every two days of business training that cultive8.com delivers, we commit to delivering one of our youth courses to a local school or community youth project, free of charge.

For more information, contact us via **www.cultive8.com** or **mail@cultive8.com**